While every precaution has been taken in the preparation of this book, the publisher assumes no responsibility for errors or omissions, or for damages resulting from the use of the information contained herein.

LET'S HELP YOU SELF-HELP!

**First edition. June 23, 2020.**

Copyright © 2020 Anthony Jacob Braaten.

ISBN: 979-8223849506

Written by Anthony Jacob Braaten.

# Let's Help You
# Self-Help!

# An INSPIRATIONAL, **PASSIONATE** Handbook for *Your* Path

by anthony jacob braaten

This handbook is a kind gift from

______________________________________

and is presented to

______________________________________

May you be inspired and filled with

# passion!

# Inspired by
# Hannah Michelle Braaten

&

# Passioned by

## Cheri Ellen Marie Braaten

This handbook is dedicated to those who are now saying,

## "HELP!"

and special thanks to those who *did* help me.

Hello, friend. Before you read what's before you, I just recommend having a journal with you to take notes, and answer self-reflecting questions. I also just wanted to let you know that I am not a doctor of psychology. I am not a guru. I am not a monk. I am not anyone of authority. What I am is a patient eager to get better. A patient eager to learn what brings lasting joy to one's life. I'm a patient, probably just like you. I am not perfect, nor do I think this book has *all* the answers you are looking for. What I can tell you is that I wish I had this book to read when I first started this path to recovery ten years ago. This book is basically "how to be happy 101." I wrote this guide in hopes of opening your mind to all the answers that can be found out there. Each section of this guide could be a book of its own. So read it knowing there is so much more out in the world to learn. This is simply what I have titled it: a handbook.

After countless sessions, meetings, and therapy, I have noticed a great pattern to what brings a person to peace. So I wrote this book. It's simply a quick guide full of everything I have gathered over the past decade, since my diagnosis with bipolar I, PTSD, ADHD, a psychotic episode, and other mental illnesses. Patient-to-patient or human-to-human, I write this all with true sincerity. If you follow this book, you will reach where I am at. My hope is that you will find lasting joy and peace and perhaps surpass me in success, "success" according to your own definition. Thank you kindly for considering this book and believing it may help you. It *will* help you, but as you read, you'll realize it's entirely up to you how much you get out of this. Have an open mind, and enjoy getting better! Peace and wellness be with you as you read.

Sincerely,

Anthony Jacob Braaten

**Write in your journal some goals down that you wish to get out of this handbook.**

# The Skills

"Just believe in yourself. Even if you don't, pretend that you do, and at some point, you will."
— Serena Williams

Hello again, friend! I'm very glad you have decided to read this. It means you are *trying*! Trying, my friend! Yes! You are putting in some effort to get better. Starting to try is extremely difficult because trying something new is always challenging, but your first step is to pick yourself up and begin. You're undertaking a scary, fabulous journey in learning about *you*! All you have to do with this guide is give it a little taste and see the wonderous things it can bring into your life. Trying is the "skeleton key," the root of everything you're about to read. An attempt is all this book needs from you. If you feel like you have failed after trying your absolute best, be willing to try again. Don't give up! You will grow to believe in yourself because you are becoming a better you. My friend, I'm so proud of you already! I'm proud of you for trying. Trying something over and over again is "practicing." You may not do as well as you wished the first, second, or even seventh time. It's okay because with practicing more and more, you will develop a new skill. And who doesn't want new skills?

***In your journal, jot down some goals you haven't tried yet, those things you may have been procrastinating on. Write them down, and see them on paper.***

The skills you'll acquire after practicing what is written in these pages will change you. They will reduce anger, depression, and anxiety; help you find yourself; and simply change your life for the better, *according to you*. Practice the twelve skills mentioned in the table of contents. Start with the most familiar or developed skill so your first challenge will progress more naturally. Don't give in to discouragement. Push yourself to keep trying. Give yourself a nice polish, get up, and shine, and believe me, friend, you will certainly shine! You just need to believe in yourself. If you went no further in reading this book, I would want you to know the importance of believing in yourself. For those who continue to read on, thank you kindly for believing in me.

*What is your definition of "success?"*

The skills I want to guide you through are only some of many, but I've chosen the twelve that I believe will promote balanced living and success. I see "success" as having peace of mind and being filled with joy over what I have achieved. I have named the skills "Willpower," "Love," "Gratitude," "Forgiveness," "Kindness," "Exploration," "Adaptation," "Limitation," "Expression," "Creativity," "Contribution," and "Passion."

*Without understanding them yet, on a scale of 1 to 5, rate what you think your level of expertise is on each skill. 1 is the lowest level of expertise, 5 the highest.*

Willpower __________

Love __________

Gratitude __________

Forgiveness __________

Kindness __________

Exploration __________

Adaptation __________

Limitation __________

Expression __________

Creativity __________

Contribution __________

## Passion __________

These skills are not in any particular order, and nor are the sections in this guide. You may have these skills already, but it may be wise to further finetune them. The skills are not a pass-or-fail test. It's important to not feel as though you are failing in *all* the skills if you believe you are failing in one. The point is that you are practicing these skills, in spite of any failure or disbelief that they are worthwhile. My friend, these pages before you are worth your valued while. These skills are worth your time.

# Questions to Ask Yourself Each Day

- In what way have I shown **willpower** while doing something I didn't want to do?
- In what way have I shown **love** to myself, another person, my world, or the Universe?
- In what way have I shown **gratitude** for who I am, what I have and haven't done, and what I do and don't have?
- In what way have I shown **forgiveness** to myself, another person, my world, or the Universe?
- In what way have I shown **kindness** to myself, another person, my world, or the Universe?
- In what way have I shown **exploration** of something new about myself, another person, my world, or the Universe?
- In what way have I shown **adaptation** to my circumstances and to any new discoveries?
- In what way have I shown **limitation** to appropriate boundaries?
- In what way have I shown honest and thorough **expression** of myself to another person or the Universe?
- In what way have I shown **creativity** that benefits myself, another person, my world, or the Universe?
- In what way have I made a positive **contribution** to myself, another person, my world, or the Universe?

- In what way have I shown **passion** while doing all the above?

# A Friendly Reminder

The key to this book is to simply try your best in all the areas set before you. You will seemingly fail at times, but it is important to remember hope is not lost. You can try again and again as long as you do not give up. This book is for quick understanding of grand topics. Use it for reference when you are in a crisis, not knowing what to do or how to act. Read deep, breathe it in, and decide to enjoy your experience. Don't hesitate to laugh at the difficulty of your first, second, or seventh attempts. I have learned to laugh at myself often during my first try at my projects and practices. Laughing is a skill of its own and is better than the alternative, which could be losing your temper or, worse, giving up entirely. It's important to me that you remain patient with yourself.

<u>Note to A Friendly Reader</u>

On the next page, and following each section is your "Champion's Log." This is simply a journal section set aside just for you. Write whatever you wish on these pages.

# A Champion's Log

# The Skill of Willpower

"The question isn't who's going to let me; it's who is going to stop me."
— Ayn Rand

Y'all ready for this? Yes, me too! Before we begin, ask yourself, "In what way have I shown **willpower** while doing something I didn't want to do?"

***Finish the sentence. I have shown*** *willpower* ***today by...***

Have you pushed yourself at all today? Have you walked across those burning coals to get to the other side? If you haven't yet, it's okay; you still have time. I ask this because at more than one time in my life, I didn't push myself the way I should have. If I had to wake up earlier than I desired, I would develop a sorrowful attitude and would not want to put in a full day. My only thought would be to take a well-deserved nap. I would shut my brain off to the world and just dream. With this attitude, you will find, as I did, that you will sleep your life away.

I have struggled with many of the same weary disorders you may be going through. I have walked across the burning coals to get away from depression, anxiety, PTSD, bipolar I, and more—whatever may push a person to reach the end of that burning hot path. Believe me when I say that this is not an easy journey. It's a battle. It's a war. It's an art. It burns inside and out. However, the path is a simple one, though difficult to master. When you get through the fiery walk—and with effort, you will—you will feel like a champion. Victorious!

Keep in mind that these skills are about you. You only need to push yourself to attain lasting results. You will find that inner strength you have been missing and start putting your **willpower** into effect. You are *allowed* to better yourself. Who is going to stop you? Not you! Not this time! Because you are a champion, right? Yes! I knew it. It is a pleasure to meet you, champion!

***Name a time when you got in your own way and were unable to reach your goal.***

All of us need to put in great effort to succeed. If you do the work, you will be left with the ability to succeed in all your challenges. Try and move toward success each and every day. It's a mental workout; I'll be the first to tell you that! Yet each day you'll have more **willpower** and be more prepared to begin your brand-new life. Change your thoughts to "I am able" or "My worth is high." You are the only person who can be *you*. (No one can take over your body and do things for you. It is *up to you*, my friend.) Tell yourself, "I will push myself to become the better me I want to be." Then do it!

***Write down something positive you would like to hear from someone you*** *love*. ***Then tell yourself that same thing.***

Successful people often say that the best things in life don't come without work you must put in. In my opinion, self-motivation and self-control are two of the most difficult skills in life. Some are born with them or develop them young, but I did not. I had to practice pushing myself until I developed the **willpower**. Try not scratching an itch (a microscopic pain) for a moment longer than you would like to. It might drive you bonkers, but what you're doing is far greater than most can do. Well done! You have further improved your ability to push yourself, increasing your self-control and self-motivation. The more you push yourself through battles that induce pain, discomfort, or fear, the more you build your **willpower**. Pushing yourself every day makes you tougher than you were, rather than weak and fragile. Yet, you are not weak or fragile. No, you're a glorious warrior! Right, gentle reader? I believe so.

***Check the box below if you have mastered self-control.***

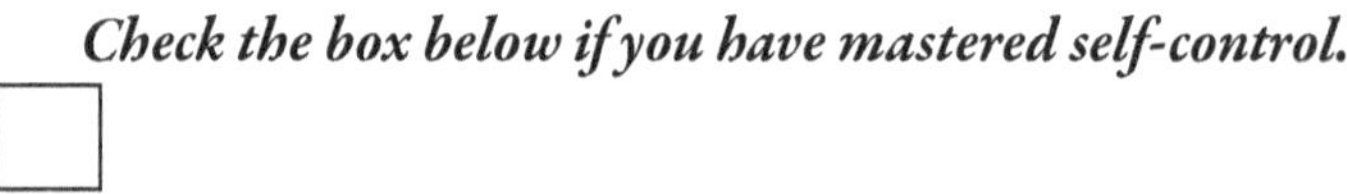

Not scratching an itch is an interesting practice in itself, but not necessary for every goal in life. It may not be an important feat for you. However, not scratching an itch immediately is finetuning the skill of pushing away an impulse and having control of your mind, body, and spirit. Having this control or awareness is sometimes referred to as "mindfulness." Mindfulness is a mental state achieved by focusing one's awareness on the present moment while calmly accepting thoughts, feelings, and even body movements and sensations. If you feel angry, notice how your body reacts. Are your muscles tense? Are you seeing red? Consider whether you were looking for a reason to be angry in the first place. If you are searching for a reason to be angry, you certainly will find that reason, I assure you. Also notice how your body reacts to happiness. Is it comfortable? Do you feel excited? Becoming aware of all your body is telling you is a great practice of mindfulness and a therapeutic technique used by doctors to treat patients everywhere. Meditation is where they usually start.

***Take a moment to jot down how every part of your body feels in this instant.***

Meditation is where you are focused on one thing at one time. It is usually done in a seated position while concentrating on posture and breathing alone. You can also center your awareness on one sentence or word as you breathe. You may repeat the phrase "I am a warrior champion," "I am stable," or "May I be well." There are multitudes of meditation practices that you can use to train your mind into believing what you are telling yourself. You have spent your entire life wiring your brain a certain way. Now it's time to untangle these wires and reassemble them into a positive and healthy pattern.

After practicing a great deal of mindfulness or meditation, you will find it easier to pay attention to your surroundings in this busy world. You will begin to live in the moment, not the past where all the ugly things reside. Mindfulness helps you accept yourself and treat yourself as your best friend. Being present in the now is and should be the main goal of all your endeavors.

***As you have been reading this guide, where has your mind wandered? Write down a few unrelated thoughts that arose while you read. Then try to focus.***

A plethora of mindfulness practices are available, but it's difficult at times to be mindful of one thing when all you feel like being is angry, depressed, scared, etc. These negative emotions can be considered mindful as well, but the goal is to be filled with positivity or, at the very least, neutrality. When you are angry and you find it unpleasant, sometimes it seems impossible to focus on something else. You just don't feel like being happy. Well, how about at peace? How about becoming so mindful at any given moment that you rarely get angry in the first place? This is possible, my friend, with the proper effort. It's possible even for the ones who think their minds are so out of control that there is no hope for them. Do not fret. You *will* have success, angry or anxious friend of mine. Just keep practicing. Using **willpower** to focus only on your breathing is a mindfulness practice one can do anywhere, anytime, and in any state of mind.

I will briefly describe one way to concentrate on your breath. You breathe in through you nose, filtering the air, and exhale through your mouth. Try to have your belly rise as you take these deep, healing breaths. The Buddha is commonly seen sitting cross-legged, mouth open and grinning, with a huge belly. What is being portrayed is a man at the peak of a healthy deep inhale, causing the belly to rise as he is about to exhale his joy and gifts of wisdom out into the world.

When someone is having a panic attack, the common reaction is to tell them to breathe and remain calm. The idea is to get this panicked person to stop thinking of what's causing the stress and only think of breathing. Breathe in life; exhale life, joy, and peace. As my mother says, "Breathe in the flowers, and blow out the birthday candles." The person will feel the panic start to melt away. Anyone who suffers from these attacks should practice breathing much like a football player practices: all week, for hours on end. The player practices the same play over and over so that when the game comes, the player is prepared. Apply this to mindfulness practices, especially breathing. Practice focusing only on your breath as much as you can. Breathe like the warrior champion you are, my friend!

I like breathing as a mindfulness practice because it's always there for you. In another breathing practice, you can take deep breaths through your nose and out through your nose. Breathe in and breathe out, filtering the air, while you tie your shoes, drive to work, and make breakfast—even while listening to a rambling fool you wish to escape from. If you like, you can even think of something positive as you inhale and exhale. Inhale and think to yourself, "May all be well." As you exhale, think to yourself, "May I be well. May I remain in the present." These are called mantras, and they can be any simple phrase you find that gives you what you lack. If you're an angry person, you can think as you inhale, "May I be at peace," and exhale thinking,

"May I believe I am not an angry person." While doing this, notice the sensations that occur within your body. Notice any tension and let it rest. Notice any good feelings and be **grateful** for them.

*Take a moment to write down a simple mantra or two you may find beneficial, and then try to use them daily.*

You can change your attitude and focus on anything just by giving yourself a little push. Willy Wonka once sang, "If you want to view paradise, simply look around and view it. Anything you want to do, do it. Want to change the world? There's nothing to it!" If you find yourself regretting the past or fearing the future, then look around you. You can achieve paradise by using your **willpower** to choose a new outlook or attitude. Remember you're always in the present moment unless your mind wanders elsewhere. If it does wander elsewhere, this is okay. Just like clouds in the sky, your thoughts float by. Don't let them make you frustrated. Simply draw yourself back to the present gracefully and kindly with no self-punishment. Notice the sky and its wonderous beauty. Feel **gratitude** for your hands and how much they do for you. Feel **gratitude** for your heart and how it keeps you alive every moment. Notice the colors blue, red, or green wherever you go. Think of three positive things that are present in your life to bring yourself back to the now.

*Take a look around at your world, at others, and at yourself. What sensations are you experiencing in this moment?*

Only think of the past for learning lessons or for reminiscing about good times once had. Only think of the future for making plans to achieve whatever goal you wish to achieve. Don't fear the future; embrace and respect it. Don't regret your past; share the lessons learned from it. Continue to live in the present.

"Want to change the world? There's nothing to it," is only a bit of an exaggeration by Willy Wonka. You're changing the world simply by existing. You have no clue of the domino effect you can have on a stranger's life when you just smile at them and say, "How do you do, stranger?" People look sad most of the time. You are needed to smile for those who don't. Become a smiling champion! Your recklessly abandoned positivity is required in the field of life. We all need *you*. You can make a change one person at a time.

You don't know what the future holds because it doesn't exist yet. The past doesn't exist anymore either, just your flawed perception of it. All you have is the present. Oh, how exciting it is that time progresses and we have the opportunity to grow! The present time and place are all you have, so make the best of it. Why think about how Sally should have said this or why Bob didn't do that? All it does is stir up strife and confusion by putting Bob and Sally in your negative mental jail where they cannot grow and keeping you from focusing on truly productive, exciting thoughts. Stay in the present. As you read this handbook, for example, you are living in the now. So, great job practicing mindfulness thus far, champion!

Many studies have shown that we are happiest when we are focused on one thing instead of an assortment of things. Matt Killingsworth, psychology major, author, and expert on happiness, believes if you want to be happier, all you have to do is live in the moment. In Matt's TED talk about his study on happiness, he states that "People are substantially less happy when their minds are wandering than when they're not." Practicing mindfulness all the time is the key to lasting joy. How can you be upset if you're not thinking about what is making you upset? You can't.

Find a goal you wish to accomplish, as simple as tying your shoes if you don't know how. Push yourself using **willpower** to learn how to tie them. Once you have done this, your shoes are tied, and you can now run. Yet, don't forget the concept of "baby steps." Baby steps are for people like you, me, and everyone else. We all must take them. They are comparable to the fable "The Tortoise and the Hare." Slow but steady wins the race. If you took a shovel full of dirt from your backyard and did this every day, you would soon have a decent-sized hole. Do it for years, add a little concrete, and now you have a gorgeous swimming pool for all to enjoy. This takes time and effort. The pool does not build itself and certainly not in an instant. You must use **willpower** to take steps toward that end goal.

Baby steps, in my opinion, are a little more complex than "slow but steady." It's a natural progression for us to grow. A baby becomes tired of crawling and understands naturally walking is better. It's what everyone else is doing. A baby must take that first step, which may be a simple discovery or an intentional action. It may be fun, but most of the time, it is a treacherously scary first attempt. However, you cannot deny that those few steps taken are a few steps taken. So keep it up! Suddenly and without expectation, the baby stumbles and falls. The baby may think, "Hmm, maybe I'll just crawl the rest of my life. It's too scary to try again." But no. The baby must walk. You must push yourself, or you will never see that green grass on the other side. You will fall or relapse. It's inevitable. It's important to know this, my friend. You must have it engrained in your mind that failure is just a part of life. It's also important to know that this failure doesn't have to be miserable. Keep trying. Keep taking steps forward with full knowledge that there will be roadblocks ahead. Be prepared to fall so the fall isn't so treacherous. Soon, you will run and leap over the roadblocks from before, though you must invite in the reality that there is always something you don't expect.

***Write about an area of your life where you are afraid of taking the next baby step.***

At the end of this guide, you will find many mindfulness activities to choose from in any idle moment where you might be tempted to think of the past, present, or future with a negative attitude. Always remember that the treasure you find may not be the treasure you were seeking. There isn't always gold at the end of the rainbow, just the start of a new rainbow. So enjoy your colorful journey and let your goals be rewarding for you. Push through the hard parts as needed. If you think you are significant, then become noteworthy. If you want to be special, then take the steps needed to be special. It usually means work, which may be why you haven't magically done it yet. Without **willpower** and action, your dreams are just sentimentalism or delusions of grandeur. There are no musical montages in life where we suddenly become good at something. Everything takes practice, so practice positivity.

But then again, champion, you are unique in your thoughts and actions. You are a special person because of this, and I hope you know that you are certainly grand. These practices are for you to become an even *better* you. It doesn't work like magic, though in retrospect, it looks that way. You have to put effort and **willpower** into new challenges. You are still becoming who you are meant to be. To do your part, you must take action for yourself. Otherwise, you will not grow into someone more special.

# <u>A Friendly Reminder</u>

The purpose of **willpower** is to get you closer to your goal. Set up a goal and work **passionately** toward it every moment you have to spare. Push yourself to practice mindfulness at all times. Do not let your mind wander, but do not be too hard on yourself if it does. Do not be afraid of failure; be afraid of never trying in the first place. Always breathe intentionally. Work hard toward your goal of becoming this special you with achievements worth noting!

## A Fascinating Fact

Argon is a trace element in the air that we breathe constantly. It has not changed since its beginning. This means we are breathing in something that all humankind has breathed before. Our lungs thus effectively touch countless people's lungs from the beginning of time until the end of time. We touch what history has touched and what the future will touch simply by breathing. We're all connected. So exhale argon covered in life and joy. Some people measure their life by how many breaths they have taken just like we do with the mileage on our cars. Take each breath in with sincerity and intent.

# A Champion's Log

# The Skill
# of Love

"All that you are is all that I'll ever need."
— Ed Sheeran

Before we begin, ask yourself, "In what way have I shown **love** to myself, another person, my world, or the Universe?"
***Finish the sentence. I have shown*** *love* ***today by...***

To **love** yourself, someone, or something is to have no wish to change it other than to help it grow into something more beneficial to its own self. You are a garden. If you **love** your garden, you water it. If you *don't* **love** your garden, you pull it up and either give up or start over. If you **love** your garden, you protect it with chicken wire and give it proper sunlight. If you *don't* **love** your garden, weeds grow, eventually killing your garden. If you **love** your garden, you add plants or ladybugs that help it become fuller and more diverse. At the end of my days, I wish for my garden to look much like a rainforest: full of life and growth. This same analogy can apply to yourself, others, the world, and the Universe.
***What does "love" mean to you?***

It is important to **love** yourself. It's close to impossible to show true **love** to others if you do not **love** yourself. If you don't **love** yourself, then it's time to convince yourself you do. Convince your heart, mind, body, and spirit that you **love** them as though they are separate from you. Much like you must convince your romantic partner that you do in fact **love** them, do the same for yourself. Tell yourself "I **love** you!" and prove it with **passion**!

*Take some time to write down things about yourself that please you. Write at least five positive attributes.*

You should "**love** thy neighbor as thyself," but if you *don't* **love** yourself, you should probably stay away from your neighbors until you do. This is a joke, of course, but the point is there somewhere. You should always surround yourself with positivity, but how can you be a positive person if you don't **love** yourself?

To treat yourself like a garden that you **love** is a balanced way to live. Give yourself proper nutrients. Drink water—but try to refrain from too many sugary drinks. You don't have to completely rid your life of sugar, which would be nearly impossible for me, but it is important to not overindulge. Use the **willpower** you've built to resist partaking in something you want over what you need. If you give your garden too much, it begins to grow those nasty weeds you hate so much. So **loving** yourself means setting **limitations**. Much like chicken wire, this guards you from harm. This book is not about heart, liver, or pancreatic health, but it is well-known that too much of anything can be harmful. Set up a defense for yourself.

*Take a moment to examine and write if you have anything in your life that you could cut back on for the sake of your health.*

Do not be mistaken, gentle reader. It is good to enjoy the finer things in life. Indulge. Partake. Pamper. Test. Taste. Drink wine if you can handle it. Party it up. Have a good time. Grow. Experience life. Treat yourself like you would treat your romantic partner. Go out for a night on the town, baby! Watch a scary movie with some scrumptious popcorn. Mmm...popcorn! Set aside time to spend quality moments with yourself.

***Name some things you would like to treat yourself to. How can you love yourself today?***

Do the things you enjoy. For example, I enjoy crafting of any sort. If I'm feeling down, I will build something new. If I see my wife feeling down, I investigate what is wrong and try to resolve the problem by being what she *needs*, not what she wants. It might just be a break from the monotony or stress life can bring. Some people play the guitar, crochet, garden, or play with their pets. For **loving** couples, lovemaking exercises of many sorts are mindful activities as well. At the end of this guide, you will find a list of different healthy activities to indulge in so you can **love** yourself while also practicing mindfulness. How nice it is to focus on something you **love** to do! Taking care of your needs first then striving for your wants later is **loving** yourself.

***List some things you* need *vs. things you* want.**

To **love** another is like **loving** yourself. If you **love** someone, it means you wish for them to **love** themselves more and to nurture their path. You don't want to encourage someone to partake in too much sugar with you. Have some sugar with each other from time to time, yes. But if you want to overindulge, it isn't **loving** to pressure someone else to do so with you. It's a human idiosyncrasy that when we are doing something we know to be wrong for ourselves, we tend to want others to join in. I suppose it's because we want to feel less shameful for our partaking.

This always reminds me of the story of Adam and Eve eating the fruit of knowledge of good and evil. In the Bible story, they both believed it to be wrong, but because they both wanted the fruit, they neglected their **love** for each other and hurt each other in the process. (Side point: Many argue it was Eve's fault that humankind fell, but the Bible clearly states Adam was standing or sitting with her the whole time, probably just as tempted to do the wrong thing.) Eve wanted so badly to eat the fruit, and it was delicious, but it also cost her a great deal. Like overindulging in sugar, Eve should not have offered the fruit to Adam but should have encouraged him to make a good decision. Adam the same.

Yet, guilty pleasures love company. How many times have you ordered French fries only if another would eat some too? This is cheating, champion, and we both know it. You are doing something you know you aren't supposed to and bringing someone else down with you. It isn't very **loving**. Of course, French fries are extremely delicious, so I can't blame you.

*List things in your life, other than French fries, that you may bring others down with you in order to enjoy.*

Here is what I think **love** is. **Love** is everlasting and unconditional; otherwise, it's just infatuation or a deep crush. It does not give up when times become unpleasant. **Love** is the very essence of patience. It doesn't want what it doesn't have. It is pleased by its very nature. If you **love** someone, you don't campaign around saying you are better than them. **Loving** another is having a mind open to their needs and the desires of their heart and not being too lazy or stubborn to help fulfill those things. If you think one way and your **love** thinks another way, then meet in the middle and see what the fruit is. I **love** blue, and my wife **loves** red. So, we blended our colors and we made purple. Compromise. See what the two, three, or eleven of you can **create**! It usually turns out to be a work of art with diverse colors.

***Finish this sentence. One time, a loved one and I compromised and created...***

To **love** somebody is to not lose your temper with them. If you have a child that you **love**, you do not scream and yell at them because they are not listening to you. You have patience and gently and tolerantly explain to them why they should look both ways before crossing the street. Children later resent the "because Mom or Dad said so" routine. It definitely had a negative effect on my life in terms of rational reasoning and providing an answer to friends—I couldn't tell them "why" because it didn't make sense to me at the time either. You later learn for yourself that cars come passing by at any given moment. It's **loving** to explain that in ways your **loved** one can understand. Let your children understand why and not just what's what.

***Examine a time in your life where the "because Mom and Dad said so" routine affected you negatively.***

Failing to compromise or to fully explain yourself can result in a **love creation** of little success. If you believe red is final and red is what it's going to be, then you don't **love** the other, and you will be left alone with no blue or purple. Don't force yourself on anyone. It isn't **loving**. **Love** doesn't say, "Me first!" Yes, you must **love** yourself fully, gentle reader, before you can fully **love** another, but it's a balance of both of you getting what you need. Meet in the middle. **Create** something awesome together. It's a truly beautiful thing to see where my wife takes me when she takes the lead. I tend to imagine her like the eagles from *Lord of the Rings*, and I trust her path knowing I can defend whatever she chooses. It really doesn't matter what you do; it's simply awesome doing it together. Try painting one side of a picture and your partner the other side. Share and receive. Play and **create**.

***Finish the drawing and see what we can create!***

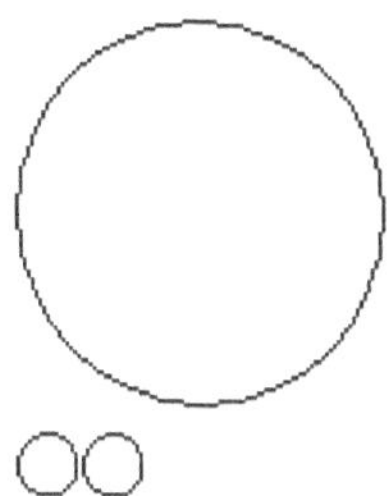

**Love** is also **forgiving.** I have been in many toxic relationships where, instead of a discussion, we always seemed to escalate the situation into an ugly argument. We both kept a checklist of each other's wrongdoings instead of **forgiving** each other. Stop keeping score, my friend. **Forgive** and forget; better yet, give and forget. Stop saying, "Well, I did this for you, and you didn't do anything!" Wash the dishes because the dishes need doing or out of sheer kindness, with no selfish agenda, not to earn points. If in an argument, champion, discuss one thing at a time. Stay level-headed. Take this dialogue, for example:

Sally: *You hurt my feelings when you check out other women!*

Bob: *Well, you hurt my feelings when you check out other men!*

This is an example of score-keeping. Bob felt justified to make a negative response, but a **loving** relationship would look more like this:

Sally: *Did you just check out that woman over there?*

Bob: *I'm sorry… Yes. I know it isn't right, and it's a bad habit. I will work on it because you are the only woman for me. I **love** you.*

Sally: *I **love** you too, and I won't check out other men either. Let's work on this together.*

Both partners have done something to hurt each other, which is common, but what is even more common is the way they argued in the first dialogue. Instead of recognizing the other's pain, a blame game began. "Well, you did this, so that's why I did that." This isn't **love**. Keep no record of wrongs if you say you **love** someone. **Forgive**, though you don't forget. You don't grow from things forgotten. Learn from each other.

**Love** doesn't get excited when a **loved** one fails. This can happen because of jealousy or because you don't **love** yourself enough. I **love** my brother Nick, I do, but I also take great pleasure when he loses against me in competitive sports. He's just so darn athletic. Defeating my dear brother in a game of ping-pong is perhaps one of my top ten joys in life. *Not* because he is failing, but because I have achieved a great feat! Nick Braaten should be a professional ping-pong player, and it is an honor playing ping-pong with him. My point is, in this game of life, **love** doesn't rejoice when the other is failing and crawling on their hands and knees in sorrow. Help them back up with **loving** support.

When you **love** your garden, you are excited, motivated, and overjoyed when it grows and bears its fruit (or vegetables). The same goes for a **loved** one. When they **explore** a new truth or accomplish their goal, you should show the same joy they do. When you see somebody grow, you share in the happiness they have for themselves because you know the effort they put in for their personal garden to grow.

**Loving** someone is never giving up on them. Be patient and endure with them with a happy heart through **thick** and thin, sickness and health. **Love** endures forever and is the cure-all for all relationships. **Love** is the light that pierces the darkness. Learn to **love** yourself out of your darkness so you can **love** others with your light. If life were a game, which it ought to be viewed as, I believe **love** is the grand prize.

**Love** your life in the same ways you **love** yourself and others. Be **grateful** for what you have been through because now you have so much to share with what you have learned. As they say, "Sharing is caring." **Loving** life is having a full life. If you **love** life, you will nurture it with activities, goals, relationships, lessons, and adventures. Take pride in the fact that you exist and are in the perfect place. Like a gear in a clock, your function is to be you. Without you living and **loving** life, the clock may not keep time on the dime. If you fill your life, you make bigger impacts in others' lives and make them fuller as well. **Love** that you exist. I **love** that you exist because you are another space traveler with me on this ship we call Earth. We all have struggles, and I **love** you, champion, which is why I'm writing what I'm writing.

Take interest in and **love** other people, trees, bugs, fish, birds, kitties, and even tarantulas. They all play a part in your life, and **loving** them will open doors you didn't even know were there. Philosopher Allen Watts points out something interesting: the deeper you go into

**loving** life, the more doors you go through only to realize there wasn't a wall there in the first place, just a closed mind. Keep your mind open and **explore** each new journey waiting just for you.

For the sake of reaching a larger demographic, I will change the word "God" to "the Universe." Coincidences, accidents, serendipitous events, patterns in nature, and random occurrences can all be credited to the Universe. It is important to **love** it for what it is. You shouldn't try to change it even if you could. We cannot change what has happened, but we can change what will happen by changing our choices. Attitude is one of those choices.

> ***Besides your attitude, what else in your life can you choose to control?***

Choices may seem overwhelming and not under your control. It has been said that the only thing you can control in life is your attitude. So, choose a positive one. There are many unfortunate people who were born into horrific locations and circumstances, but that's out of anyone's control, especially yours, my friend. One should try not to hate these hard beginnings once they've escaped these hells. Be **grateful** for your escape. I was born into a privileged life. I have struggled with so much guilt about it. I shouldn't feel this guilt, however; I should **love** my life because it's part of who I am. I should share it. I should use my gifts to help. Those with unfortunate circumstances should do the same. Use your gifts to help solve the problem or at least develop a map to help others like yourself out of the labyrinth. **Love** should be somewhere on that map.

This whole handbook is the map I've developed to keep myself out of the labyrinth within my mind. My goal is to help you escape the lies, lies like "I am nothing" or "I am not worth anyone's while." I want you to find that authentic truth that belongs to you. You will find it if you try to **love** yourself, another person, your world, or the Universe. Expect a change in your heart. Expect wonderful things to occur. **Love** yourself, then **love** others, and do it again tomorrow. I'm here to cheer you on.

# A Friendly Reminder

Why **love**? Well, it's much more fun on this side of the fence. I've been on the indifference or hate side of the fence, and it is not nearly as great. Don't get me wrong: while **loving** is beautiful, it can also be full of sadness and pain. You cannot allow that to stop you. Choosing to **love** is not an easy task. You are making yourself open and vulnerable to hurt, sadness, and possible letdown. Still, be brave and join in from the **loving** side of the fence. **Love** yourself like you would **love** another. Being

gentle and **kind** is an **expression** of **love** in all cultures. **Love** is our greatest power as humans. Be that **loving** hero you want to be!
A Champion's Log

---

The Skill of

# Gratitude

**"Gratitude** turns what we have into enough."
— Anonymous

Before we begin, ask yourself, "In what way have I shown **gratitude** for who I am, what I have and haven't done, and what I do and don't have?" ***Finish the sentence. I have shown*** *gratitude* ***today by...***

It is time we started focusing not on making ourselves great again, but instead making ourselves **grateful**. There was once a time when people were **grateful** for what they had, have, and will have. This is definitely rare in today's society, especially with the negative effect social media can have. We are constantly comparing ourselves to others we deem more fortunate and wishing we had what they have. We should be wishing we had the joy that they may have. Instead, we wish we had all the materialistic pleasures and fame. **Gratitude** starts simple with an examination of your life, but turning that into a **grateful** attitude will take significant practice.

***Can you list at least ten different things in your life you are*** *grateful* ***for?***

"I wish..." is a phrase I try to refrain from saying or thinking too much. **Gratefulness** is a mindful skill that lacks annoyance or aggravation. If you say, "I wish...," you are obviously not **grateful** with the present. You'd prefer something different. Perhaps you'd prefer something you have previously fantasized about, or you are experiencing something you had before that brought displeasure. If so, I am sorry that you don't have what you want, dear friend. Remember that a healthy examination of oneself is a mindful meditation on what you do have, performed with the attitude that you are pleased it isn't gone. You are thinking about what you *do* have instead of what you *don't*.

***Can you name just one wish?***


Jealousy is a green-eyed spiraling-downhill monster that grows and grows until it consumes you and you become full of resentment and loneliness. Be content with what you have, or if you must, strive to achieve what you do want in a positive, healthy, and peaceful way. Refrain from jealous thoughts. Those thoughts are worthless and a waste of your precious thought-life.

***Are you jealous in any way? What is it you're jealous of? How can you refrain from obsessing over this jealousy?***


Every year, as family and friends, we go around the Thanksgiving table and say one thing we are **grateful** for. By the time we are through, there is usually about twenty of us that say, "I'm **grateful** for my family and friends." This is good and **loving**, and all seem to appreciate the tradition. It tends to leave a warm, fuzzy feeling. When the rare person says, "I'm **grateful** for my house" or "I'm **grateful** for my car," this is good as well, but it doesn't leave that warm, fuzzy feeling unless you know what that person went through to obtain those things. If you know Sally was homeless and Bob had to ride his old bike 20 miles a day, you might start to feel for their stories. You might even shed a tear. (It's quite all right for a gentle warrior like yourself to shed a tear once in a while.)

After high school, I went downhill. I lost my identity and didn't truly appreciate who I turned out to be until somewhat recently. I had spent a great deal of my thought-life wishing I could be like I was in high school: wholesome, **creative**, hilarious as can be, and **passionate**. After effort and time, I discovered that I am *still* wholesome, **creative**, hilarious, and **passionate**, just a little more seasoned. I wasted a lot of time wishing instead of being **grateful**. Spending time thinking of all the time you've wasted is a waste of time. In some ways, I wish I knew that in my early 20s, but I am also **grateful** I didn't know. This is the part that is difficult for most: appreciating or, rather, respecting your past. You have been through quite a few trials, friend, and so have I. We're still alive, and you can still read or, at the very least, listen. Maybe you're depressed that it is raining, but this must happen in order for your favorite wildflowers to grow. Show love to your past self, but also **kindly** say, "Goodbye." You will never be your old self again, but you can practice becoming who you want to be now, step by step, little by little, and leap by leap.

*Try to think positively for this next question. How are you different than you were in high school?*

This is where you take inventory so you can become more **grateful**. Gather in your mind everything you have done in your life, wrong or right, good or bad. There is no proper format to this (I suggest writing it down), but be respectful of your past, your present, and your future aspirations. Our perspectives of ourselves can turn askew over time, so be honest when you write these things down.

*List all the good deeds you have done in your life. Take pride in what you write down.*

***List* all *the things you think you have done that would be considered a "wrong decision."***

***Write down your bad deeds and your regrets. Be careful when doing this, as it will bring up emotions.***

What follows is my attempt to remedy one of my greatest mistakes. This apology will give both me and the people I'm apologizing to the chance to move on. I believe this is one of the most crucial parts of this entire book: apologizing when needed after self-examination.

By my senior year of high school, I was so burnt out by football that I wanted to quit, but quitting was not an option. I took my car and purposely wrecked it in a dirt field to get out of football practice. It didn't work. I ended up being completely fine, without a scratch on me. So, I made up the excuse that my inner ear canal could rupture if I continued to play. I stood on the sidelines full of shame and guilt for having done something wasteful, careless, and downright nuts. Unfortunately, my Ford Mustang didn't make it out alive. Not trying my absolute best at football that year is one of my biggest regrets in life. I still have dreams where I've missed many football practices, and I wander around the high school trying to avoid contact with my coach.

Though the shame and guilt haunt me even to this day, I practice trying to feel the opposite. I've learned to take this story and turn it into a success instead of a failure, because I've never done such a thing again. I learned something. I grew. I am **grateful** I know not to put myself through that again. I tell people how I made an intentional sharp right turn into a vacant dirt field at 70 mph, flipping end over end with no seatbelt, just to get out of football practice, and they tend to laugh their heads off and love me even more for it. They wouldn't laugh if I hadn't learned, though. My dad still hasn't laughed. If I'd continued this behavior, I would definitely have been hospitalized as a danger to others and myself. I'm lucky to be alive.

***Write down any excuse you may have made up to get out of
something you didn't want to do.***

To feel better about yourself, hopefully gain closure, and simply do the
right thing, search through your past for all that you feel you have done
wrong, and if it doesn't cause any harm, apologize and **forgive** yourself
so you can move forward and nurture **gratitude**.

***Is there anyone to whom you feel you owe an apology? Write those
apologies down and send them in the best way you can think of.***

I'll take this platform to sincerely say this to my former football coach
and teammates whom I feel I failed: "Coach, fellow teammates, I'm
so sorry I failed you in the past. I wish I had listened to you all about
showing up and following through because that is all life is about.
Thank you for trying so hard with me. You are all kind and giving men,
and I didn't show you the respect you all deserved. I am truly sorry and
full of more regret than you could possibly know. I hope this reaches
you all. May you be well, old friends." There! I feel better now, and I
hope this reaches them in the way my heart wants it to. I am **grateful**
there is such a thing as **forgiveness**. I am **grateful** I have learned my
lesson: to push through and endure.

From here, you move forward. If the person you wish to apologize
to doesn't accept your apology, know you did your best to remedy
what you feel you destroyed. In Catholicism, this may be thought of
as confession. In the twelve steps to recovery used by Alcoholics
Anonymous, this is the fourth and fifth steps. What this does is help
you let go of the past and grow and nurture **gratitude** for the lessons
learned. It also refreshes your perspective of yourself. If you bullied
someone, they may not want an apology from you, so in this case, get

it off your chest. Tell a supportive friend of your regrets, or, at the very least, write them down, and then move forward.

***If you have done something that you think is unforgiveable and have no one to tell, write it down in your journal.***

Respect your past so you can respect yourself now. Be **grateful** in the now and have a positive attitude about your current situation because it definitely could be much worse. My friend, **gratefulness** is all one needs to carry on with a positive attitude. How can one be ungrateful and full of joy at the same time? It just doesn't mix. A mantra I used to recite in my head over and over was, "I am **grateful** that I am great!" Doing this certainly changed my attitude toward life by giving me a joy and self-appreciation I never knew of before that. My friend, it's time you learn you are a great person, but until you know this, remain **grateful** for who you are now. Be **grateful** you can read, breathe, examine, play, and do whatever else pleases you. Be **grateful** even in the hard times. Someday, hopefully soon, you will find your **passion** as I have. You will find your path as I have. You will find yourself as I have. Be **grateful** you have the opportunity to choose to be **grateful**.

# A Friendly Reminder

Exercising **gratitude** in self-examination can be done any time. It is a good use of your time if you are feeling jealous or unsatisfied. Set a goal, push yourself toward it, and achieve a **grateful** attitude. Taking inventory of all that is you is difficult, but very therapeutic. Get to know yourself tremendously better and be **grateful** for what you have. Share what you're **grateful** for with others. Be **grateful** for the difficult lessons you may have learned. You are now stronger and more seasoned. You are a beautiful, amazing warrior champion!

## A Fascinating Fact

An assortment of successful people enjoy what is called a "vision board." This board has a time stamp on it such as "I want to be here in ten years" or "Here's what I want to do before I die." They often hang these vision boards in their bedrooms, restrooms, or even their offices to have a constant reminder of their goals. More often than not, these boards manifest into reality, almost like magic. These boards often change over time, which is exciting, too. Look up vision boards online and see how **creative** people can get. Doing this will give you a better idea about yourself and help you manifest your destiny. Make your own and see where it leads you!

# A Champion's Log

# The Skill of

# Forgiveness

"**Forgiveness** is the fragrance that the violet sheds on the heel that crushed it."
— Mark Twain

Before we begin, ask yourself, "In what way have I shown **forgiveness** to myself, another person, my world, or the Universe?"
***Finish the sentence. I have shown*** *forgiveness* ***today by...***

My dearest reader and friend, I had much difficulty writing this section. I hope it reaches your heart as I intended.

Dr. Fred Luskin, author of ***Forgive*** *for Good* and one of the leading experts on the science and art of **forgiving**, says, "So much of **forgiveness** is being able to chill." Relax, everybody! Or as Kendrick Lamar says, "Be humbo! (humble) Sit down!" You can't relax if you are holding on to something that causes stress, anger, grief, pain, any sort of suffering. According to my dad and some others, "The number one killer is stress." This is just one reason to **forgive**. **Forgiving** is moving on from the stress of reliving a painful history by remembering it in a positive light. So much of **forgiveness** is having a humble, compassionate, **loving**, and **grateful** heart. There are many angles to **forgiving**, and you must remember, especially for a particularly difficult circumstance, that it is a process to let go of the past and grow from it.

***Write of a time when you were*** *forgiven* ***for something you wanted*** *forgiveness* ***for. What feelings occurred when you were*** *forgiven?*

You have a stray cat that you wish to **love** and care for. You reach to pet it. The cat bites you and then scurries off. You can either hiss and bite back or understand the situation for what it is. The cat is probably scared and previously had an abusive owner. If you **forgive** the pain of the bite, you will reach out and attempt to pet the dear kitty again. It may claw you this time. Continue **forgiving** and growing, and eventually, this feral cat will become tame. This analogy can be broken down into many different steps of how to **forgive.**

***Think of a time when you*** *forgave* ***something or someone. How did that feel?***

Why **forgive**? It's unpleasant to suffer the same story over and over. To **forgive** isn't necessarily forgetting, because how can you grow from what you have forgotten? You can't just ignore what has happened to you. You must be willing to grieve in order to **forgive. Forgiving** is an action where you look at the past differently and hopefully with a positive perspective. At first, you must try to understand what it is that has happened. With the cat, you can understand it had no bad intention toward you personally. A cat is simple to **forgive**, but people can be a more complicated case. The practice of not taking things personally with others will help you understand and practice **forgiveness.** Understanding your circumstances and theirs will remove the negative thoughts and create positivity. The instinct for the cat was to defend itself. You probably wouldn't take that too personally. Try to ignore frivolously rude words toward you, and your perspective will change.

The following three paragraphs are especially difficult to write because they involve people I **love** dearly. The two people in this story of true **forgiveness** are both men I respect. This story is not intended to rehash old difficulties or instill a remembrance of strong dislike. This story is simply a firsthand experience where I had to **forgive** someone I didn't want to **forgive**. The act of **forgiveness** was easy once my perspective changed, and my spirit was relieved.

**Forgiveness** gives one freedom to look at the disputes of the past with a healthy perspective. Here's the experience I'd like to share with you. I witnessed a dearly **loved** man, well-respected by all, especially me, getting beaten and kicked by a man I also **loved**. The older gentlemen did provoke the younger man to anger, but physical abuse is not the way to solve anything. There are many better ways to handle anger, especially if you are twice the size of your opponent. When your anger rises to an uncontrollable state, remove yourself to collect your thoughts and composure. This will prepare you to have a civilized discussion with a goal of resolving the situation.

In my eyes, the younger man deserved a good old-fashioned beating himself. I don't believe in violence personally, but it seemed justified at the time. I began to hate this younger man for something that had happened years ago. I couldn't fathom how someone could do such a thing, especially to this older man everyone **loved**. I had a growing hate toward the younger man, and it became difficult to converse with him after everyone seemed to have forgotten what happened. Not **forgiving** him was eating away at my very soul as I replayed the incident over and over in my mind. These negative thoughts ruled over me, and eventually, the hate became a mental prison I locked the younger man in. When you do not **forgive** someone, you don't give them the opportunity to grow in your thought-life. Without **forgiveness**, whoever is locked in that mental prison stays the same way in your perspective despite the many efforts that person may be making to better themselves. It was time I **forgave** this younger man for my own sake because this younger man used to be a friend whom I held in high regard.

I've come to forgive this younger man and, surprisingly, **love** him almost as much as I **love** the older man. How? I look at the situation differently now. Nothing excuses the action, but understanding the situation differently helps me accept what occurred: a mistake made in a state of rage and **passion**. The younger man could have been considered a bully at one time. A bully usually has some sort of deep, underlying self-esteem issue. They pick on those they deem less than them in order to feel better about themselves. It's very sad to see this happen. The younger man hated himself and thus took it out on others, especially those who were similar to him in ways that he disliked. The older man has **forgiven** him, the community and I have **forgiven** him, but do you think that he has **forgiven** himself? I hope so, but probably not completely, because he truly adores the older man just like everyone else does.

I wanted to avenge my old friend, but fighting the younger man would just worsen his probably already miserable mental life. What good would it do to beat someone while they're already down? Still I sense self-hatred, but his issues are diminishing while his self-confidence is growing. He may not have completely **forgiven** himself yet, but he has since become a **loving**, kind, gentle giant who has raised two very wholesome children with his wonderful, supportive wife. He has since taken a vow of no violence, something I respect highly. Because I know how I feel about my past poor decisions, I know he still must struggle with what happened. I **love** this guy now, so much that I ache for his pain, having to live with the mistakes he had made. A mistake is all it was. I hope his heart can **forgive** him and also me for holding a grudge against him. He certainly deserves to **forgive** himself. He has transformed and probably would never have if it weren't for **forgiveness**. I wouldn't have a friend whom I've learned much from if I hadn't **forgiven** him. My ugly thoughts toward him have disappeared. Because I look at the situation differently now and have grown, I do find myself forgetting it ever even happened. I'm sure most, including the older man, can say the same. He has become a very **loveable** guy. The older man, younger man, and I still talk, and they are doing better than ever. All because of **forgiveness** and understanding.

All this can relate to the cat story. Because of constant **forgiveness,** the cat remains a part of your life and is **loved**.

***Check the box below if you have ever*** *forgiven* ***someone you did not want to*** *forgive.*

☐

It was my choice to hold that man in the prison of my grudge after everyone had already **forgiven** him. I didn't have to pledge my allegiance to this suffering by saying, "I will *never* **forgive** him for this."

***If you are holding a grudge or have pledged to not*** *forgive* ***something, then write that situation down and see it on paper.***

I didn't have to feel this negativity. I did have to grieve, but once I accepted what happened, I could choose to either let it go and learn or sit in anger and boil until I exploded. To be free of the suffering, you must grieve, accept, and then move on. As I said at the beginning, this takes practice. Grief has five stages (denial, anger, bargaining, depression, and acceptance), and you must go through them, but hopefully, you can come to that fifth stage, acceptance, and then move to **forgiveness.** Going through the grief stages may make you feel an assortment of emotions. Do not block out these feelings. Notice them and let them pass naturally. I want you to learn to **forgive** and accept your past. It will allow you to be free to live in the present. I'm urging you to **forgive** so you can give little thought to a negative past.

I do my best to **forgive** as soon as possible before my thoughts put me and those who harmed me in that mental jail. As much as I like to be **forgiven**, it's an awesome opportunity to be someone who can easily **forgive** too. **Forgiving** is magical. I don't like to keep people in a jail for something they did years, months, days, or even moments ago. There is no room for growth if I hold a grudge against that person. Say Sally said something so sour that you held a grudge against her and have to **forgive** her to move on. If you don't **forgive** Sally, it might sour everything she says thereafter. What if Sally had no knowledge she said something sour? What if she was just having a bad day? (Perhaps you were having a bad day as well.) What if Sally could bring new joy to your life just like the younger man did to mine? You would never know until you let go of what she said. Move on. Grow. Be a **grateful**, open-minded individual, and it's much easier to **forgive** another. Be a **grateful**, open-minded, and **forgiving** individual and see how easy it is for you to be **forgiven** in return. This will fill you with **love**, and people will **love** you right back. Your path in life will change. Animals, plants, and the Universe will treat you **forgivingly** as well. Everything will simply flow like a peaceful river for a **forgiving** person.

*Have you placed someone close to you in your mental jail for something they did in the past? Write those people down and see them on paper. Be careful when doing this, as it can stir up unpleasant emotions and memories.*

Now we move on to subjects of greater intensity. My heart breaks for those who have suffered through unthinkable evils. Those unthinkable evils we tend to not like talking about. It bothers me so much that these nightmares occur, things of evil intent without remorse. The thought of **forgiving** someone so evil seems impossible. How can you move on? I'm not entirely sure. But I do believe it is possible and very therapeutic to move on. What I have gathered from people who have **forgiven** such evils is that **forgiving** that evil person will set you free of reliving that moment or time period. It holds you in a prison of suffering and reliving that part of your life if you don't **forgive**. Someone very close to me was beaten countless times and molested as a child. This person always says, "Do not let the evildoer win by remaining a victim gripped with fear and brokenness." Rise up above the situation and eliminate the problem the best you can. **Forgive** and become fearless. **Forgive** and be healed of this brokenness. You will rise above the trauma by grieving, accepting what has happened, and then moving forward to be the beautiful, strong, amazing champion you are. You may never know why this happened to you, but you will be an overcomer of your traumatic experiences.

I also suggest counseling and sharing with others. Nobody should have to go through these trials alone. Share how you've overcome the struggle of "Why did this happen to me?" Horrible things happen to people who don't deserve it, and I don't understand. But I know that we can make a choice to make the best of a situation. Those who have gone through situations such as yours somehow move on and **forgive**. There is hope for you. You may find that people who have not suffered in any great way can be a little shallow when it comes to helping you. Yet, you who have struggled and may still be struggling are filled with compassionate skills that can be used to help other victims who are suffering. You are who you are because of the pain you have endured. You are not helpless or weak. You are among the brave who continue to press on and try to make the best life for themselves. You are stronger than you know. You are an overcomer who is prepared for the next trial. Again, it's a process of suffering or grief, then acceptance, then **forgiveness**, and then growing and sharing. Help others who are stuck in the past to move on as well.

*Check the box below if you are an overcomer of trauma, brave one.*

☐

To move on to a more abstract point of view, I will guide you through how to **forgive** the Universe. This brings us to the beginning of this section. Relax, chill, and show **gratitude**. The Universe is always on my mind, so when I stub my toe, my first reaction is, "WHY, GOD?! What is the point of this pain and suffering?!" My best explanation is that there is a reason for all things that occur. You can either blame the Universe and its magic, or you can simply take it for what it is. It's up to you. The reason I stubbed my toe is because I wasn't being careful. If I learn to be more careful, I will not stub my toe. It's a lesson from the Universe to be more careful—or maybe it's just normal consequences. It's up to you to decide that. Ask yourself if you believe in the perfection of where you are currently. If you do, it's extremely inspiring! If you don't, then you are in the same boat I used to be in. Then, I watched *Les Misérables*. The story shows you how bad things occur. The story also shows you how those bad things fruit good things in the future. I believe it rains so that flowers will grow. Bad things happen so we can have the opportunity to grasp the brighter side of things. This does require us to use our **willpower** to make changes so that everything works out—it won't just work out on its own. But because you have experienced a straight line, you now know what a curved line is, too. It is raining, and it's miserable in the moment, but looking forward, this will help your garden grow. If you view every mishap as an opportunity to grow intellectually, physically, or emotionally, then you are wise.

Looking back, you can either be dumbfounded by life's beauty and its perfect inner workings or you can spit on its troubles. I say be dumbfounded. Life is beautiful when you look at it with **grateful** eyes. You must go with the flow of life's circumstances.

*Spend some time thinking of your situation in life. See if it is something you can forgive. Write it down.*


There was a Big Bang (perhaps "Let there be light!" was spoken), and many years later, here you are. If anything were slightly different in this explosion, you would not be who you are today. There is something called "the butterfly effect." This phenomenon, in reference to chaos theory, is that a very small change in a complex system can have large effects elsewhere. If any one of these dominos were to be slightly moved, the effect would be entirely different. Think of your experiences as some of these dominos. They may seem unimportant or unnecessary, but they are part of your future and present made by the past. We are a glorious alignment of dominos or stitching in a quilt. Find it to be beautiful as much as you can, my dear friend. Be excited that you are alive and playing a part that will go down in history. It's exciting because as one of these dominos or threads, you have many choices. Let your choices be wise, selfless, and **loving** in order to add ample artistic designs to your life. Don't be impatient. Your opportunity will come, and you will know it without a doubt. It takes time, but you can **create** many opportunities for a new domino to fall whichever way you want it to whenever you want.

Practice **loving** the Universe as you have practiced **loving** your garden. Take care of it. Contribute to society. In the Bible, in God's first sentence to Adam and Eve, he tells them to reproduce and prosper, but he also says to govern the Earth responsibly. So, take care of our Earth. **Forgive** our ancestors for polluting and making the world the way it is now, move forward, and contribute to life on our planet in a positive way. Go with the flow. Volunteer. Pick up trash. Recycle. Compost. Use paper over plastic. Carpool. It's simple and can be invigorating to live this way. I don't know why but I find great pleasure in having my recycle bin fuller than my trash bin, though I should refrain from so much consumption.

**Now think about the world's condition. Write down the things you don't like about the world and see them as something you also have the opportunity to** forgive, **even as you strive to make things better.**

**Forgiving** the Universe is more difficult for some than others. This is because some of us have nice lives with little struggle. Those people are probably not reading this guide. They don't need it or want it, and they do not understand why people like us do. There are those who naturally balance themselves, lead successful and joyous lives, and never seem to show any sort of struggle. Sure, they may struggle with money or impatience from time to time, but have they really struggled as much as you and I have? Maybe, but probably not. I've noticed a game of sorts that people play in life, especially in the self-help and recovery community. The game of "My Story Has More Struggles Than Yours,

Which Is Why You Have It Better Than Me and I'm Still Struggling

More Than You." People long for sympathy and understanding when

they've tried their best and failed. Offer it to them. People need **love** in

a world where it may be hard to find. If they need to feel they are worse

off than you, bite your tongue (not too hard, champion), and let them

be reassured that they are worse off than you. Don't play this game

yourself. Respect your past, yes, but do not flaunt it to show you have

it worse. Everyone is different, but people are the same in many ways.

Find those similarities that are negative and eliminate them. Become

unique in your suffering, unique in the fact that you are willing to

**forgive** your past and make the best of it. Learn from your past and

share real stories of importance. Don't tell stories of how miserable you

are because of something that happened years and years ago. Don't be a

complainer. Nip it in the bud now with grief, acceptance, and moving forward. Guardian of triumphant tales, gentle reader, friend, beauty

anthropomorphized, tell a victorious story!

# A Friendly Reminder

Do not be so stubborn that you cannot **forgive**. Really try to use your **willpower** to **forgive** something or someone. Understand that you must *grieve* if you are hurt, but try to consider all the circumstances of the event and come to a better understanding of what took place. Accept what has happened and willingly cut your losses. Then move forward quickly. I hope you can **forgive** because it's just another power we have as heroes. Just like with **love**, being a

**forgiving** person makes it easier for others to **forgive you.**
A Champion's Log

# The Skill of Kindness

"How **lovely** to think that no one need wait a moment, we can start now, start slowly changing the world! How lovely that everyone, great and small, can make their **contribution** toward introducing justice straightaway... And you can always, always give something, even if it is only **kindness**!"
— Anne Frank

Before we begin, ask yourself, "In what way have I shown **kindness** to myself, another person, my world, or the Universe?"
***Finish the sentence. I have shown*** *kindness* ***today by...***

As Anne Frank once said, we can start now in slowly changing the world with **kindness**. Believe in yourself full-heartedly by being **kind** to yourself. Be **kind** to yourself even though you may think your mind is sick. Why do we trust ourselves when we say negative things about ourselves? Why? Even worse, why do we trust a negative person who tells us those same things? Sometimes it seems that it would take an army of positive reinforcers to make us believe differently. Help this army by telling yourself positive things. You are wise. You are gorgeous. I hope these words affect you because they are very much true. If someone approached my wife and told her the same negative things that she tells herself, I would have a difficult time holding back my anger. These words that my wife tells herself are killing words from someone else. Why is that? Why is a negative word so much more powerful than a **kind** word? Perhaps because we tend to believe the negative more often than not. This is a poor practice and a destructive exercise. Thinking negatively, especially about yourself, is a bad habit people tend to accidently fall into and master. If you're constantly thinking that the glass is half empty, then you are going to get very good at thinking that way. **Kindness** can make someone's glass half full.

*Can you come up with five kind things you could tell yourself right now? Try to tell yourself these kind words anytime you are filled with self-doubt.*

There are those with confidence, and there are those with low self-esteem. People with low self-esteem have mastered the art of telling themselves they are not good enough. Confident people have a skill foreign to the misinformed people with low self-esteem: positive reinforcement. Sometimes this positive reinforcement that confident people carry within themselves can be misinterpreted as being cocky or prideful. If you're confident because of all the **kind** things you say to yourself, start spreading that confidence to others with a **kind** word. I have a close friend who is confident but who could come across as prideful to strangers. My friend picked up something heavy, something I could not pick up. I said in astonishment, "Bobby! How are you carrying that?!" and he confidently replied, "Because I'm a freaking hog!" It made me laugh and think in agreement, "Yes, he is a hog." He didn't say he was stronger than me and that I'm weak. He simply stated a pleasant truth about himself. There's a difference between haughty pride and confident pride.

*Can you name at least one person who is confident and has been kind to you? You should try to spend more time with that person.*

Confident people find it hard to understand people with low self-esteem. They don't understand how someone could be so downright cruel to themselves, basically killing themselves from the inside out. The responsibility lies within us all to be **kind** to one another, but I believe a confident person has more power to change someone's negative thought into a positive thought. Confident people are powerful, so practice being **kind** to yourself to become confident.

*Define "kindness" in your own words. What attributes does a kind person have?*

**Kindness** is an **expression** of **love**. **Kindness** is humankind's superpower. A gentle touch on the shoulder, a hug, a smile, a flower, a surprise gesture or gift, or a positive word can save someone's life. It is within our power to be **kind** to ourselves and **kind** to others. This is exciting! You have the power to heal deep emotional wounds. You have the power to encourage someone to do great and wonderous things.

*If you could do something kind for your past self, what would it be?*

Bill Gates tells a story of when he was a younger man who had to take a plane flight. He had no cash on him at the time and wished to have a newspaper to read. He addressed the paper man at his kiosk and explained the situation, promising to pay him later. This same vendor helped him twice over the course of a couple of months. His **kindness** impacted Gates significantly. Nineteen years later, Gates found this man again and offered him whatever he wanted. The man replied, "I helped you when I was a poor newspaper vendor, but you are trying to help me now when you have become the richest man in the world. How can your help match mine?" Gates, in an interview, comments, "People need to understand that the truly rich are those who possess a rich heart rather than lots of money. **Kindness** makes you the most beautiful person in the world, no matter what you look like." I agree with him.

This vendor also had integrity. He didn't showboat his **kindness**. It was just a simple thing to him that he ought to do for anyone. **Kindness** should be a simple task. Don't be afraid to be **kind** to someone for fear of making things awkward. Be **kind** according to your personality and character, and don't force it. Let it naturally come.

We don't know what an act or word of **kindness** will do in someone's life. Sure, we can say this act of kindness led to Gates being comfortable on a plane ride, but I'm sure it meant more than that to him. Someone was **kind** to him. It's unforgettable. This event stayed in Gates' mind for decades, and he was willing to give a fortune for the act of **kindness**.

What do you think a negative act or word would do to someone in that instant?

*Has someone ever been kind to you without payment in return?*
*Write that situation down.*

The pen is mightier than the sword! The tongue is like a double-edged sword; it can penetrate deep with either **kindness** or cruelty. Put your shopping cart away in the shopping cart return. Put unwanted items back in their proper place instead of where it is convenient for you. Don't flip off a stranger who cuts you off on the road. Leave a place you've been staying the way you found it, if not better. Be a **kind** person whenever and wherever you can, even though the only reward is your own knowledge that you were **kind**. This will boost your self-esteem.

*Check the box below if you return your shopping cart to the shopping*
*cart return when finished with it.*

I used to be a barista working for the great and powerful Starbucks Coffee. My favorite challenge of the job was defeating people with **kindness** despite their overwhelmingly rude behavior. I never once received a complaint from a customer. People **loved** me there. Then one fateful day, I added a little too much foam to the latte of a customer who had requested extra foam in the first place. This customer was a regular, and I thought we were friends. Instead of approaching me, he placed a complaint saying I was rude and made his coffee wrong. No reprimand took place because of my reputation, but his negative comment stuck with me. It irked me so much I had to put him in this book. All is **forgiven,** however. Later, we became gym buddies, and we remained cordial with each other. My point is that words and gestures are powerful. This small instance has stayed with me like a haunting.

There are two reasons I think all Americans should work in customer service. First, it's a blast because of all the strangers you get to interact with. Second, people need to know what it's like to be servers, cashiers, etc. The fact that they are so mistreated boggles my mind because these people are handling your food. Treat others **kindly,** especially those in customer service, and you just might brighten their day, which in turn may brighten yours.

*Check the box below if you are among the brave who have worked in customer service.*

If you are **kind** to your garden, science shows it will grow healthier and fuller. You've heard of people reading to their plants? Well, there's actually some reason to that! IKEA did an experiment involving negative vs. positive reinforcement. Two identical house plants were placed in symmetrical locations in an IKEA store. In front of the plants were instructions for customers who walked by. Both instructed shoppers to not touch the plant. One instructed the customers to say something negative to the plant. The other instructed customers to say something kind to the plant. After just a month, with no other variables than the ones mentioned, the bullied plant withered and died. The plant that received positive reinforcement thrived! It was amazing! We have superpowers, people! I'll quote Uncle Ben from *Spider-Man* here: "With great power comes great responsibility." I believe it. Each of us have the power of the word or gesture. Smile at others. Wink at others in a goofy way. Make people feel like they mean something. Tell them a positive thing. If someone thinks they are an idiot, tell them they're brilliant and give examples. Do the same for yourselves and be honest. Say **kind** words to yourself!

***Check the box below if you are a champion who has withstood the test of being bullied.***

Say someone is being negative to you, and you already have a difficult time being **forgiving**. Try something a little in the grey area of morality. Defeat them with **kindness**. Nothing shuts a negative person up better than something **kind** said about them. It's also hilarious to see how people react when they're ready to do some fighting and all you want is peace. Of course, two wrongs don't make a right. So, be sincere with your **kindness**.

*Can you describe a time when you defeated someone with kindness and felt at peace with how you handled the situation?*


Lastly, be **kind** and **loving** to yourself. If you tell yourself you're an idiot, then that's how you're being an idiot right there. You are not an idiot. I know this because you are seeking to better yourself. Tell yourself you are the opposite of your usual negative thing. Don't say to yourself, "I'm a failure." Say instead, "I am victorious over many battles!" Be **kind** to yourself, your children, strangers, animals, and plants, and you will be a superhero.

## A Friendly Reminder

Just like everything else, be as **kind** to yourself as you are to others and the Universe. Being **kind** is a power we must use instead of the power of cruelty. Our words are like a double-edged sword. Our cruel words can cut deep and cause permanent damage, or our **kind** words can penetrate deeply into someone's heart and change them forever because of an unforgettable act. Time to unpack those positive adjectives and send them into existence!

# A Champion's Log

---

# The Skill of Exploration

"The important thing is not to stop questioning...One cannot help but be in awe when he contemplates the mysteries of eternity, of life, of the marvelous structure of reality."
— Albert Einstein

Before we begin, ask yourself, "In what way have I shown **exploration** of something new about myself, another person, my world, or the Universe?"

***Finish the sentence. I have shown*** *exploration* ***today by...***

I recommend the movie *Blast from the Past* to help you understand this section a little better. I'll briefly explain its premise. The story is about a boy who is raised from birth in a fallout shelter by a wholesome, mild-mannered couple who mistakenly think a nuclear bomb has struck. The boy lives in isolation with his eccentric scientist father and old-fashioned momma for 30 years. He becomes a gentleman, knowing much about science, arithmetic, art, boxing, history, proper etiquette, and the morals of the 60s, but nothing of the outside world. After 30 years, the son is sent out into that world. The comedy shows how this man **explores** the wonderous things the world has to offer. In one scene, he sees the ocean for the first time, is filled with overwhelming excitement, and begins a full-blown sprint to jump in. The way he reacts in the ocean makes you want to jump right into thrilling new discoveries as well. Throughout the movie, he finds all sorts of things he never knew before and becomes giddy over them. It's one of my favorite movies because I believe we should all act this way. We should always be gentle but childlike when it comes to our **explorations**.

*Can you describe a childhood memory where you were excited to try something you had never tried before? If you lost it, then where do think this childlike hunger for exploration went? What changed in your life to make you less inquisitive?*

We should constantly be on a **passionate** exploration of new objects, ideas, activities, and adventures. All it takes is looking around you. Why settle for the isolated fallout shelter you are currently trapped in? **Explore** the world and what it has to offer, and do it with that childlike **passion**. **Explore** like your life depends on it. You may find something you never knew existed, just like the man in the movie.

When I used to go to church, my pastor would tell a variation of the same sermon at least once a month. Hilariously, people grew tired of this sermon, but I **loved** it. I think he told the sermon so much because he believed he couldn't get the point through anyone's closed-off minds. I'll sum up the story for you: Chris grew up very poor, eating simple foods like noodles, hot dogs, cheeseburgers, etc. After he had dated his future **loving** wife for a spell, it came time to meet the in-laws. He was nervous and wanted to impress the family. His wife-to-be at the time informed him that her brother made the best guacamole in town and that he must try it. Chris, never having had guacamole nor anything else the color green, was terrified. He thought to himself, "I'm going to avoid this guacamole as much as I can!" When they finally reached the future in-laws' house and were greeted at the door, there stood his future brother-in-law with a chip already scooped in hand. Chris had no choice but to eat the guacamole-loaded chip right at the front door. Then Chris realized something about himself he had never known. Chris loves guacamole! He puts it on everything now, and he tries all sorts of foods he never would have tried in the past. A whole new world of flavors opened before him. You never know what you love or don't love until you've tried it.

*Do you have a similar story in your life where you put off trying something, then finally did, and ended up loving it?*

I never knew I liked writing so much until I sat down and tried it. Now I write every day. I never knew I liked tabletop board games until I gave them a try. Now I play all sorts of games we discover as a family and friends. I love the saying from *Forrest Gump*, "Life is like a box of chocolates. You never know what you're going to get," but I always add at the end, "Unless you keep buying the same darn box of chocolates!" It's good to experience the unexpected, but if you keep doing the same things in your world, you should expect the same outcomes to occur.

Be engaged in constant **exploration** of new things in your life to perhaps open a door to a new **passion** or to the path your life is meant to take. This is one reason why we take an assortment of classes in elementary, middle, and high school. We take them to open our minds to the possibilities that are out there for us to **explore** and **love**. The grass is greener somewhere, so go find that side and see if it's something you want to dive deeper into.

One key to searching for a new idea or way of life is by examining the attributes of close friends. It has been said that we are an average of the people we hang out with the most. This is partly true. We do things with our friends because we enjoy the same things. It's best to have an assortment of friends to broaden the possibility of adding something new to your world.

*If your life were a book, who would be the central characters in this book? Write their names down and see how they have formed you into the person you are today.*
*What would be the title of this chapter in your life? Who are the central characters in this chapter, and what influence are they having?*

My cousin, who was an inspiration for this section, is a strong reader. He is constantly reading so he can open his mind to what's out there. He is a full person partly because of his reading. He has **explored** what works best for him. He has **explored** who he wants to be. He's one of the most open-minded people I have ever met, accepting of all walks of life. I attribute that to his adoption of the character attributes seen in the stories he reads. He becomes the average of the characters he **loves**. So read and read some more! If you're not much of a reader and you find it hard to sit still, try audiobooks or watch informational YouTube videos and movies of high culture. **Explore** other people and what makes them tick, because what makes them tick may make you tock.

*Think of your favorite character. Write down their attributes that you find pleasing. Write down their morals.*

You can **create** and mold yourself into whoever you want to be. Just because someone may be a fictional character doesn't mean they are not real to you. Let the positive attributes of your favorite character shed onto you. Meld with them if they fit into your life

For a time period, my **passionate** exploration, which was obsessive, depressing and a little self-destructive, focused on the meaning of life. I struggled to navigate through a labyrinth of my own creation as to what is right, what is wrong, and why. Why must we exist? What comes after we die? If God exists, why is there so much ambiguity? I hit a dead end; yet, on this adventure, I found myself. The treasure I was looking for turned out much different than the one I found. I concluded that the purpose of life is to **explore** and then share with others what you've discovered so you can all have enjoyment after your efforts. Find your individual purpose, not somebody else's purpose, and fulfill it.

If your purpose at this time is to make coffee for customers that come into your shop, then smile and get to know their drink of choice. Make that sweet cup of joe like it was for the queen. Be **passionate** about your time and place because you never know the domino effect you will have on this world. That smile, coffee, and **passion** could be for the next Gandhi or Mother Teresa. You just don't know what the future holds. Why think that you do? Try your absolute best in what you are doing here and now, regardless of whether you have found your purpose yet. You will find something to **explore**, I assure you. Be aware of and **grateful** for the treasure that you now have, even if it's different from what you imagined or hoped for.

*Have you ever found something different from what you expected*
*that was still positive and pleasing?*


You can be whoever you want to be, but it's less exhausting to be the *real* you than it is to be a fake you that reflects how others may want you to be. **Explore** who you want to be and build upon the you who already exists. Be a full person ready for infinitely more.

*Can you list the attributes of that one, true, authentic you?*


The wisest people say, "I know nothing," because what they know doesn't compare to how much they don't know. **Explore** here. **Explore** there. **Explore** everywhere, my friend. I can't say it enough. Don't tell yourself, "Eh...there's nothing out there for me to explore; everything is boring." Trust me, you have *not tried* everything! There is so much the world has to offer, so once you find that guacamole, scarf it down like a champion after battle. Be the child who's never had ice cream. Lick it, savor it, eat the whole thing. Make sure to enjoy it with others.

**Explore** within yourself the things that bother you or hold you back as well. **Explore** and destroy the negativity, and then share the good news of how you overcame a struggle. It's just as important to search for new ideas as it is to search within yourself for old, negative ideas that are detrimental to your wellness. Ask yourself, "Am I being self-destructive with this habit, behavior, or thought?" If you are, then replace it with something positive.

*What's the obstacle standing in your way to finding yourself?*

# A Friendly Reminder

Be cautious of falling into a rabbit hole of frivolous exploration like I once did. Yet, be inquisitive at all times. Do not assume you know all there is to know. Search for new experiences and knowledge. Learn what you're interested in and get started in the development of the new and improved you. Starting is the hardest part, but once you do, your self-esteem and character will grow. You will begin to enjoy your own company. **Explore** all there is to **explore** and develop your own personal opinions. Try different things, especially the things that others have already discovered they **love**. You may end up **loving** them, too. Keep an open mind and never close it off. When in doubt, read about it! Read this. Read that. Read it all. **Explore** yourself, find what you don't like, and get rid of it. Mold yourself into the person you want to be all the time.

## A Fascinating Fact

Online, you can find what is called "fanfiction." Let's say you **love** *Lord of the Rings* as much as I do, but you want more. There are countless stories kept true to the original's nature and written by fans. You can further **explore** your favorite characters anytime you want. Fanfiction is almost limitless in its content. Give it a try; you may **love** it!

# A Champion's Log

# The Skill of
# Adaptation

"A scholar tries to learn something every day; a student of Buddhism
tries to unlearn something daily."
— Alan Watts

Before we begin, ask yourself, "In what way have I shown **adaptation** to
my circumstances and to any new discoveries?"
***Finish the sentence. I have shown*** *adaptation* ***today by...***

They say it takes two to four weeks to make or break a habit. I agree.
**Adaptation** is the process of doing so. It is adding and subtracting
ideas to help you become more equipped for your life. **Adaptation** is
a survival skill that must be learned. This was my firsthand experience
with this skill.

The way I had thought my whole life drove me into an episode

of psychosis when I was 27. This episode lasted about three months,

and it had to do with the obsessive **exploration** I wrote about earlier.

In my recovery, I had to learn to **adapt** to the lot I was dealt. I had to

make a decision to not think this certain way. I was possessed by and

**passionate** about an idea that drove me to a different reality of

my own **creation**. I had to **explore** myself and eliminate the negative

or false thoughts altogether. I had to be indifferent toward them. After this deletion, I became directionless and empty. What am I to think about? Who am I? I looked to my friends, family, and coworkers to find a new way to think that would keep me from this expedition into a destructive thought-life. I had to relearn to move from an abnormal reality to a healthy reality. Some of what I learned from others worked, but some of it didn't sit right within my heart. It wasn't me. I gathered their wisdom and blended it with mine to **create** the me who would sit right. I added and subtracted over and over again. I read, **explored**, and adjusted until I felt at peace. Then it was time to expand on it and let the true Anthony Braaten come out, a proud new me who remains consistent. I do my best to remain myself regardless of the company. I want to be the same person I am to the people I **love** as to a stranger. I've made no room for an alter ego. So, as you **passionately** **explore** within and without yourself, **kindly** add to what you like and subtract what you dislike or what is getting in your way. There is always room for improvement.

*Write down some positive things you would like to integrate into your life.*

*Write down some negative things you would like to remove from your life.*

*After you have added and subtracted these things, what will your life look like?*

# A Friendly Reminder

With any time-consuming habit that is broken comes an empty time slot. You must replace it with a mindfulness activity of the same power. Replace what you do not like with what you do like. It sounds simple, but it is not easy in all circumstances. Remain your true self at all times.

## A Fascinating Fact

When you finish a task, sometimes it's hard to switch focus to start a new task. Many people who struggle with anxiety about this carry with them what's called a "transitional object." When they finish a task and need to focus on a new one, they use the transitional object to first replace the task. This can be anything: a Rubik's cube, a yo-yo, gum, your phone, a fidget spinner, whatever fits in a pocket.

# A Champion's Log

# The Skill of
# Limitation

"Respect your efforts, respect yourself. Self-respect leads to self-discipline. When you have both firmly under your belt, that's real power."
— Clint Eastwood

Before we begin, ask yourself, "In what way have I shown **limitation** to appropriate boundaries?"
***Finish the sentence. I have shown*** *limitation* ***today by...***

Boundaries are the **limits** we set with other people and ourselves that can indicate what we find to be acceptable and unacceptable behavior. **Limiting** yourself and others you come into contact with is important. Let's go into further detail. Setting up certain rules for yourself and **kindly** letting others know these rules is good practice in the appropriate setting. There's a way to let others know your boundaries. It's best shown by your actions, though at times, you may have to **express** them with words. By simply obeying the rules you've set up for yourself, you can show others where you stand figuratively and literally. For example, it's okay to tell someone who is too close to your face to back up. All you need to say is, "Do you mind backing up a little? I need more space."

The **limiting** factors you set in your life can be broken or revised by you. They are living rules that are organic and grow with you, not against you. It's important to still allow the freedom of **exploration** to take place and to allow the **adaptation** of rules where necessary. Your living rules will change over time. You should travel light if you can. If you require many extreme **limits**, this is okay, as long as it brings you peace and success. Try not to be in bondage to your boundaries.

### *Write down any rules you have for yourself.*

Some alcoholics who wish to **limit** themselves to only drinking wine eventually find it leads them to drink harder alcohol down the line and return to square one again. They eventually **limit** themselves entirely, abstaining from alcohol in all forms in hopes of achieving peace. Other addicts say the same thing. They say that you must abstain completely, quit cold turkey. Thus, we see that some people have difficulties and must put up very extreme boundaries to completely abstain from a specific action. One negative result with abstinence is that there's now an empty space where your habit once was. A time slot must be filled. What is to be done with this empty spot in your thought-life? Replace it with diversity. Your garden needs much to survive. To quit cigarettes, some chew sunflower seeds and drink water, but that can be a lot of seeds and a lot of water. You must replace an extreme habit with extreme, diverse, mindful actions. Addiction can require extreme **limits**, but diversity seems to dampen the extremes and bring more freedom for **passionate** exploration. Part of this **exploration** is learning what is most effective for you to achieve peace. Different boundaries work for different people.

A close and wise friend is not an alcoholic, but has set up a strict boundary of abstaining from whiskey because he thinks whiskey is "delicious!" He admits he will drink too much of his favorite beverage once he starts. He has committed to abstaining from drinking whiskey at all to maintain his healthy ego.

*Check the box below if you have ever quit something mind-altering that took a great deal of willpower to quit.*

Healthy personal boundaries are a balance of knowing when to say "no" and when to say "yes." Those who get too involved and those who don't get involved at all are two examples of extremes. You can have strict boundaries or loose boundaries, but well-balanced boundaries are ideal. A balanced person with balanced **limitations** values their own opinion. They don't compromise these values for the sake of others. They share private information appropriately and at the right time. They understand their needs and can **express** them to others. Lastly, they can deal with being told "no." Because they have healthy boundaries, they are confident with themselves and not easily swayed.

It is common to have a mix of strict, healthy, and loose boundaries. What's also common is having a boundary or ego change with different people in your life. Whether you are with strangers, friends, family, or coworkers, you should not change your **limitations**, but they naturally do shift until you have established what's called "integral boundaries."

Integrity is remaining true to yourself no matter who is around. How exhausting is it to constantly be changing who you are depending on who you are speaking with! Be respectful, honest, assertive, and at peace with yourself, and you should be able to be the same person with whomever you are speaking. Always have the confidence to show your true colors.

***On a scale of 1–10, 1 being very loose boundaries, 5 being balanced boundaries, and 10 being very strict boundaries, how would you rate yourself?***

You value your own opinion. _____________

You compromise your values for the sake of others. _____________

You share private information appropriately. _____________

You understand and **express** your needs to others. _____________

You can cope with being told "no." _____________

You are confident with yourself and not easily swayed. _____________

## A Friendly Reminder

Setting healthy **limits** for yourself can help you as well as others. Your boundaries keep you healthy and stable so you don't change your ego or personality from one social group to another. Value your boundaries while you let them be healthy. You will grow with integrity.

## A Fascinating Fact

If you struggle with drug addiction or alcoholism, there is *always* a place for you. Narcotics Anonymous (NA), Alcoholics Anonymous (AA), and other twelve-step recovery programs can be found anywhere at any time. They are set up to help addicts abstain from any particular mind-altering substance. The programs are highly successful in recovering their members to sanity, self-respect, and **love** for themselves and others. In these programs, typically, there is a topic of discussion for the hour, and everyone who volunteers to share does. The sharing of stories is done to reach others with similar stories and guide them to recovery. In these groups, there are so-called "sponsors." A sponsor of your choosing becomes a close friend to help guide you on your path to recovery. Each sponsor also has a sponsor above them. Wisdom is passed down and spread throughout the program in this way. Give one of these programs a try! Keep in mind it only works if you work with the program.

# A Champion's Log

# The Skill of Expression

"Silence becomes cowardice when occasion demands speaking out the whole truth and acting accordingly."
— Mahatma Gandhi

Before we begin, ask yourself, "In what way have I shown honest and thorough **expression** of myself to another person or the Universe?" *Finish the sentence. I have shown* expression *today by...*

Occasionally, speaking the whole truth is necessary. You need to get things off your chest. Why carry alone the burden of something that is bothering you, my dear friend? How nice it would be if my garden verbally told me what it needed! There is something special about **expressing** your sorrows and woes in a journal, online, or verbally to a close understanding, patient friend or an unbiased professional such as a counselor. What you're doing is **exploring** emotions and memories that bother you and why. Perhaps you feel guilty about something, and nobody knows about it. Do you really want to carry that around your whole life alone? "Alone" is the key here. When you **express** your sorrows, worries, and problems, you become less alone with that sorrow. Someone now knows about it and is now hopefully sympathetic. (If they aren't sympathetic, you may be speaking with the wrong person.) We need people. I'm sure you have all heard that a baby needs human touch to survive. This must translate in our minds as well. A **kind** word of encouragement and understanding or simply a silent listening ear is in fact touching, touching the heart and mind. It is a natural instinct for a baby to **express** itself by crying. At some point, we lose this instinct to **express** our needs. When a baby cries, it's heard by a **kind** and **loving** ear, and then is fed, held, and comforted. We need this as adults. You have a problem, and somebody else either has the answer or the comfort needed to keep you striving on. Lean on me, my friend; you're not alone.

On the subject of professional counselors, these helpful people are often avoided or misunderstood. "Ahh, I'm fine. I don't need some stranger telling me how to live my life." Too many tell themselves this, including myself before I sought help. Yes, a counselor is a stranger, which in a way is the beauty of it. You can say whatever you want to a stranger. In my experience, counseling isn't how Hollywood portrays it. I've never laid down on a couch and talked to someone seemingly disinterested and doodling on a notepad. It's usually a comfortable setting with some coffee or tea and a one-on-one conversation with a **kind**, unbiased ear. After years and years of visiting the same counselor, he is still a stranger to me because I'm not there to get to know him and his life problems. Don't get me wrong; I do know a little about him, but that's because I've grown to care for this man for all his help. What he knows about me and what I know about him don't compare. We have a professional relationship. I'm able to completely **express** myself without judgement or bias. I'm there to sort through *my* problems.

It takes time for counseling to really have a strong impact. It's akin to the snowball effect. The more you visit your counselor, the less of a stranger they are to you and you to them. It also takes **willpower** to be honest with your counselor and keep an open mind to this person whom you are speaking with, a professional there to examine you like a doctor examines a sore throat.

I once asked my counselor, "What is the purpose of all this counseling? What does it do for me? How can you help me?"

He replied, "Right now, Anthony, your thoughts are like a tornado with a bunch of stuff swirling around within it. I'm here to help you sort through that tornado of thoughts. You may have thoughts like, 'Take the trash down on Wednesdays,' 'Anniversary's coming up...Gotta plan something,' etc. Normal to-dos just swirling around like Dorothy's house in *The Wizard of Oz*. Yet, also what is swirling around is the Wicked Witch, thoughts like, 'I hate myself; I'll never **forgive** myself.' I'm here to help you **explore** that tornado of your thought-life. I'm here to help you pluck out those useless and self-destructive thoughts that terrify you. I'm here to 'pause' the tornado so we can get a better look at it in order to see what's pointless, negative, and causing the problems. I'm also here to tell you the honest truth after I've heard your mind and heart loud and clear."

I have heard another analogy for how counseling works: Your thoughts are like files in a filing cabinet. You open the drawer and can see every thought-file, but what you can't see is what's attached to each file. For example, you open one file labeled, "Groceries," but what's also attached to that file is "grocery budget," then to that file, "unemployment," then to that file, "find a good job," and so on. Imagine what files may be attached to a certain traumatic experience in your life! A counselor helps you sort these thoughts out as well as **explore** thoughts that may be mixed in with others.

***Write down any and every thought that occurs in response to the following statement: "I am enough."***

I believe counseling of some sort is for *everyone*. History shows that so many societies housed a "wise one" to seek counsel from. Why do we today seem to neglect such a necessity? A counselor is needed for "Joe the plumber" just as much as they are needed for "Eugene the panicked." If you're religious, then seek the help of your religious leaders. They are set in place to listen and guide. If you are not religious, visit a scientist who specializes in thought-life: a counselor.

You can also take Alcoholics Anonymous (AA) or Narcotics Anonymous (NA) into consideration. These are a court-mandated cure for addiction. Do you know what they do in these hourly meetings worldwide? **Express** themselves. A typical meeting consists of people going around and sharing their problems with other strangers. The program works, just as the government seems to think. But the key is to continue to practice **expressing** yourself honestly. After a typical AA or NA meeting, everyone gathers in a circle and chants, *"Keep coming back! It works if you work it!",* which hits two points. It's important to seek help, a safe place to **express** yourself, but if you don't use your **willpower** to take action, it won't work. There's such a thing as an "ask-hole," someone who asks for advice, who is then given sound advice, but who then neglects the advice. Don't be an ask-hole; be a warrior for action. There is a Bible verse saying something along the lines of "Faith without action is dead." You can believe everything in this book, but if you don't practice the advice, then close to nothing will come of it. "Keep coming back!" also encourages you to not give up. You may hear a story that relates to you and that inspires you on your journey.

It can be hard to open up and talk to someone. Studies have shown a great deal of benefit in relieving anxiety, depression, anger, and stress by writing in a journal. It's a safe form of expression, like writing to your future self. If you write in it now and read it ten years later, it's quite similar to telling an unbiased listener or someone who has your best interest in their heart. We change so much over a decade, a couple of years, months, or even an hour. Writing your thoughts down not only get things off your chest and gives you the ability to **explore** something from a different perspective, but also gives you a deeper outlook on who you are and who you once were. You can look back and see your growth.

**Expressing** what's on your mind doesn't have to be all about negative things that bother you either. You can write compliments to yourself and others or your opinions on any manner. It's important to be sure you are understood. Don't be overly cautious to speak. It all returns to simply being yourself: never changing for the comfort of others. You suffer when you're not being yourself. We are gears in a clock driven by self-**love**. **Love** yourself. Learn to **love** what others have to **express**. **Express** your opinion if so asked or if it's important to do so. Avoid frivolous negative speech.

Bob: *I hate* Star Wars.

Sally: *Why? They're classics?!*

Bob: *I don't know; I just hate them.*

Without reading Bob's mind, we can assume he's either trying to be cool and counterculture, different from others, or he simply doesn't know why he doesn't like *Star Wars*. For Sally, this ends the conversation because Bob is just being negative. Have an opinion, but know why you have this opinion. Let the opinion be yours. Be **passionate** and don't change your opinion to be cool.

A great book that changed my life, *The Four Agreements*, states that one agreement you make with yourself, given the proper **willpower**, is to let everything you say be the truth, concise, without error, and as meaningful as possible. "Let your word be impeccable," it says. Think before you speak. Refrain from **expressing** every little thing that pops into your mind. You won't be respected if you interrupt, say what you don't actually live, or speak negatively about everything. Try to picture someone you know who doesn't speak very often and is a little quiet at social gatherings. If there is an opportunity for this person to speak, usually they are respectfully heard. Sometimes what they say is very profound and uplifting. This person thinks. They gather all the data around them on each person they **love** before eventually **expressing** themselves, hoping to be of help. The fewer the words, the better. It's better to say "Be well," rather than listing off everything on how to be well and why. Just be well, gentle reader.

# A Friendly Reminder

**Express** what's bothering you with the appropriate person or group at the appropriate time and setting. If you are alone with your thoughts and have no one to seek council from, then write your sorrows and woes down in a journal. Get the negative thoughts out of your head. Make sure your words are well thought out and truthful.

## A Fascinating Fact

Some practice this as a way of saying goodbye to a problem.

They take a negative event that has happened in their life

and transfer that event's energy into an object like a stone or a piece of paper. Then, with **passion,** that rock is thrown into the sea or that paper is burned. This tends to help people say goodbye to the past and hello to a new self. A professional can provide you with other productive skills to help you say goodbye to your old unhealthy thought-life.

# A Champion's Log

# The Skill of
# Creativity

"**Creativity** drives us to not only **create** but to innovate."
— Kacey Spencer

Before we begin, ask yourself, "In what way have I shown **creativity** that benefits myself, another person, my world, or the Universe?"
***Finish the sentence. I have shown*** *creativity* ***today by...***

When you **create** something, it becomes an extension of yourself. You have used your talents to birth a new **creation**. Because you **love** yourself, you should **love** your new **creation** as well. **Create** often and be proud of anything you have tried your best to make.

**Creation** starts with coming up with an idea. Any idea will do. **Creation** can come in all different forms. Try cooking a new dish, painting or drawing, planting a garden, coming up with a game, inventing, innovating, etc. **Creating** is simply changing your environment into something vastly different. It will keep you busy and away from anxiety or depression. It is a boredom-buster. You don't want your world to become stagnant. **Creating** brings enjoyment and change. We would still be in caves if we didn't have **creation**.

We all share the feeling of **creative** envy. There are some things others can do that I will never be able to do. Focus on the things you can do or desire to do and expand on them. Something you enjoy may be **creative** already. Change it a little, and it becomes the art of your own **expression**.

***Write down something you are good at.***

Psychologist Mihaly Csikszentmihalyi wrote the book *Creativity: Flow and the Psychology of Discovery and Invention*. There, he describes **creativity** as "a central source of meaning in our lives…Most of the things that are interesting, important, and human are the results of **creativity**…When we are involved in it, we feel that we are living more fully than during the rest of life." Studies show that as children, we are extremely **creative**. As we age, we become less so. What's happened is we have stopped trying. We have become too critical of ourselves. **Creating** should never stop no matter your age. Don't let the finished product bother you. You have tried your absolute best. Be proud of what you've made! Your **creation** is from the unique you. Taking inspiration from others and making it your own is "innovating." You could in turn bring inspiration to others with your innovation.

I'm not much of an artist when it comes to realism, which is why I enjoy abstract art. I pick an emotion and try to draw it using colors, lines, and patterns. Something you **create** doesn't have to be perfect, but because it is something you have **created**, you should be proud of yourself. Just remember art in its general form is not referred to as a representation of perfection. It's an extension of the artist. Unless the **creation** is intended to be perfect, like actual space rockets, do not be afraid of not achieving perfection. Remember beauty is in the eye of the beholder. What you should strive for is a **creation** made with **passion, willpower,** and enjoyment. If you don't like your specific **creation**, then practice doing it again. Practice doesn't make you perfect; it simply makes you better.

On the cover, you may have noticed the graphic of the compass rose. This compass rose is one that I drew on my computer. It is something I've drawn my entire life, in fact. It has a much deeper meaning to me. Notice the opposing white and black circles. What I've drawn is my rendition of a compass rose and the yin and yang symbols combined. I wanted to create the image of a life fact. In life, we are in this constant state of **exploration**. We are constantly deciding which direction to go. Comparing the compass rose to life, we see many different directions we can take. When you look deeper at a decision to be made, you may notice both the good and bad sides. This is what the white and black circles symbolize. In every bad decision, there is a little good. In every good decision, there is a little bad. This is my **creation**. I've taken two things already invented and made them my own with heart and **passion**. Try taking one, two, three, or seven things and combining them to make something brand-new. Most **creations** today that we use are innovations: cellphones, computers, cars, and so much more. Things are always improving and changing.

Parents? I'm talking to you now. Encourage your children to be as **creative** as possible. Give them any medium to **express** themselves without judgment. You should take this advice as well. You will learn about your children, and your children will learn about the world and themselves. It's crucial for proper development toward their adult life. Once we're adults, this remains crucial as well. You don't have to encourage your child to be a painter or sketch artist. Maybe get them some Legos or Lincoln Logs. **Creativity,** safety, and health should be the main concerns when raising your child. There are multitudes of studies that you can investigate that show how important **creativity** is in the early development of children. Start with PBS and branch off from there. Do not dampen your child's **creativity** or your own. Show support in all your loved one's **creative** endeavors and only supply constructive criticism when asked. Do the same for yourself. Only criticize yourself if you are not **passionately** trying your absolute best.

The list at the end of this handbook includes many activities that involve **creation** or innovation of some sort.

Lastly, know that you can also **create** yourself. You can shape and form your mind into anything you want it to be with **willpower** and practice. Use the vision board method. Mold yourself like clay, gently and with **passionate** intention. When you create this new you, it will draw others near, and then they too can create a new self, having been inspired by a champion such as you.

*Using only adjectives, describe who you would like to be.*

# A Friendly Reminder

Don't be hard on yourself; just **create** something you like. Once you've done it, be proud of what you have **created,** my friend. Whatever you **create** is an extension of yourself. Something you enjoy that isn't yours can be altered by you, and now, it's an innovation. This can be done with virtually everything. Alter your coffee, just a little, and now, you're a barista! You're in the process of becoming the authentic you that you can **create**. Let it be a you that you **love**.

## A Fascinating Fact

There are two websites that are very popular today that focus on creativity. Etsy is an online store like Amazon, but all the products are handmade by individuals like you and me. There are several home businesses that produce these works of art. You can buy almost any unique **creation**. You can also open your own store on this website and sell your precious **creations**. A lot of the ideas for Etsy products come from a website called Pinterest. This is a fascinating version of the vision board idea. You can browse countless pictures of just about anything and pin them to your virtual boards. I like to **explore** and **recreate** DIY projects.

# A Champion's Log

# The Skill of Contribution

"Appraisals are where you get together with your team leader and agree what an outstanding member of the team you are, how much your **contribution** has been valued, what massive potential you have and, in recognition of all this, would you mind having your salary halved."
— Theodore Roosevelt

Before we begin, ask yourself, "In what way have I made a positive **contribution** to myself, another person, my world, or the Universe?"
*Finish the sentence. I have shown* contribution *today by...*

Now that this handbook has miraculously changed your life, it's time to **contribute** to the world. Yes, it is *always* time to **contribute** small or big things to our fellow space travelers. A **kind** word **contributes** much. A blanket or sandwich for the homeless can go a long way. Have a giving heart, and your **kindness** will be returned.
*Think of the best gift you have ever received. Write down the emotions you felt when you received that gift.*
*Think of the best gift you have ever given. Write down the emotions you felt when you gave that gift.*
Every year, my sweet momma **contributes** by buying us countless gifts for Christmas. She is hands-down the most generous person I have ever met. I'm excited about these gifts each year, but what I'm more

excited about is giving my gifts away. There's nothing wrong with the desire to receive; only when it begins to consume you does it become something like greed or ungratefulness. It's much more thrilling to give!

I hope that this handbook will change my life first, followed by one person's life, followed by the lives of millions of others. I feel the world would be a better place if people knew these skills. It wouldn't change it into a nice world but a **kind** one. There's a grand difference between "nice" and "**kind**." Nice is too giving and less thoughtful, whereas kind involves appropriate, assertive, and thoughtful giving. If we all **contribute** our part and be **kind**, then the world would be a much better place. Don't you think?

If you **love** yourself, others will **love** you. So do not isolate yourself. Spread your **love** to others. Recycle, compost, feed the homeless, donate to proper charities, be **kind** to others, pollute less or don't pollute at all, provide factual information to others about health and wellness if asked, and offer yourself to the service of life because you are a hero. It's your responsibility to **contribute** to society. Communism would only work with **contribution**, which is why it doesn't work at all. I'm not an advocate for communism, but I do believe if everyone **contributed** what they could, then the world would be a much more fruitfully **kind** place.

*Name five ways you can personally* contribute *something positive.*

Andrew Carnegie was a multi-millionare who believed you should teach a man to fish rather than give him a fish every day. He believed if a man died wealthy, then he had failed to use his money wisely. He didn't believe in free money because who should be the judge of who is worthy of that free money? People might just gamble it all away. He believed in **contributing** to society by building parks, libraries, better schools, and other communal centers. He believed in making the world a better place. I believe the same.

Everyone is fortunate enough to share. It's as easy as sharing a good laugh. If there is such a thing as right and wrong, then I think it's right to share with others what they need or strongly desire. Spread joy and happiness by being yourself!

Science shows much about giving. It releases endorphins known as a "helper's high" and is good for our health in general. Research shows that giving can drastically relieve stress. It promotes giving back as well. It's a contagious spirit. Giving also evokes a state of **gratitude** in another person's heart. Your simple **contribution** could stick in someone's mind their entire life. I recommend reading the article "Five Ways Giving is Good For You" by Jason Marsh and Jill Suttie for more information.

# A Friendly Reminder

**Contribute** positive things such as ideas, **kind** words, goods you don't need, etc. Be there for others in need. Being there for them is your way of **contributing**, the responsible thing for a hero to do. Teach a man to fish instead of giving him free fish every day. Be eager to give rather than receive. **Contribute** what you can and get that helper's high!

# A Champion's Log

## The Skill of
## Passion

"There is no **passion** to be found playing small—in settling for a

life that is less than the one you are capable of living."
— Nelson Mandela

Before we begin, ask yourself, "In what way have I shown **passion**

while doing all the above?"

*Finish the sentence. I have shown* passion *today by...*

We can all live a **passionate** life, and we don't have to accept anything less. This is where you should start getting excited since being excited is the most important point here. Living with **passion** changes your life. Before we go any further, let's see how *Webster's Dictionary* defines **passion**:

- "a strong liking or desire for or devotion to some activity, object, or concept";
- "ardent affection"; and my favorite,
- "intense, driving, or overmastering feeling or conviction."

In the words of Ramina Murshudova, an education specialist at the U.S. Embassy in Azerbaijan, "**passion** is a mixture of what you love doing and what you're good at doing." She has also stated that 87% of people are unengaged in their work. It is a problem that work is work for them, as these individuals lack **passion**. Now, let's discover your **passion**.

As you're reading this, you may be at an all-time low. You may be in a deep pit of despair and self-hatred or lost in the dark. You may be wondering how you can discover your **passion** in this state of mind. Feeling depressed or hopeless is a difficult state to experience and sometimes a downward spiral that seems impossible to escape. Yet if you motivate yourself and take those baby steps, you can get yourself out of that pit of despair and self-hatred. Never lose hope. Once you've lost hope, you're hope*less*. I believe, however, that if one can lose hope, then one can find hope as well. Believe in yourself as everyone else does. **Love** yourself, and *develop* your **passion.** You may have heard that "whether you think you can, or you think you can't, you're right," which means that if you believe you can do something, then with effort, you can; if you believe you can't do something, then the odds are that you won't because you don't believe you can. Nobody built a bridge by saying "I can't build this bridge." Say "I can" first, and then act. One of my wife's most attractive attributes is that when she's challenged by a task, she constantly tells herself, "If someone else can do it, so can I!" It's a contagious saying as I and others try to rationalize the same way. It's a motto worth adopting.

I say develop your **passion** for more than one reason. Yes, find your **passion**, but if you know what it is, then develop it. Embrace your **passion** with the highest sincerity and magnify it vigorously. Support your **passion** with **passion**. You will not always be the best, but you can try your best and take pride in knowing that you did so. The pride you experience after attempting a task with maximal effort and heart is intoxicating (in a positive way) and highly motivating for trying again and again. You begin to **love** being you. You begin to **love** life. You begin to develop **passions**, some of which you would never have thought would be **passions**. I never knew I was going to write a positive reinforcement handbook. As I tried to find answers for myself on how to be at peace, I found that

I loved sharing what I learned about life with those I **love.** I want to share what I've learned since after experiencing much depression, manic episodes, an episode of psychosis, ADHD, and other common life struggles, including "Who am I?", I've come to sit down and write this book. I've come to a place where I can share what I've learned with the world. I was filled with **passion**. I want to talk about what I've written in these pages all the time. I'm **passionate** about what's in these pages. I'm **passionate** about finding true lasting peace, and I believe that what I've written here will do that—that finishing this handbook and practicing its skills will lead me to peace.

Always do your absolute best in all your endeavors (one of the four agreements), but try your best as an enthusiast would—with reckless abandon. Try your best until your nose bleeds (not literally, of course)! Try your best without any hesitation. By trying I mean doing. There are so many reasons to live this way. For instance, I have a friend who is a bit of a fussy eater. He'll try different foods, but how he does it is hilarious. I laugh any time I see him try something new. He had never tried sushi before, so I had to convince him to try it. He was reluctant but willing. He took the smallest bite possible (as if his teeth were fingernail clippers), getting only a sliver of seaweed. He instantly cringed; yelled, "UHH!"; and spit it out. I told him, "No, you gotta stuff the whole thing in! That's the whole point of sushi!" He needed to attempt the full experience and not eat just seaweed. I believe if he had taken a proper bite, experiencing all that the sushi had to offer, he would have liked the sushi. When you try something new, know what you are trying. **Explore** all its possibilities, and as an enthusiast would, stuff your face with some delicious sushi. Get the full experience by trying your best.

**Passionately** eat that sushi, baby! After you've done so and decided that you don't like it, try it again, and then if you still don't like it, walk away. It's okay to not like something, but then you can truly say, "been there, done that." Your opinion is what makes you who you are. If you do like it or even **love** it, then expand! Try all sorts of sushi. Try making your own sushi. Be the "sushi guy or gal," and be proud of it! Say "HEY, WORLD! I LOVE ALL THAT IS SUSHI, AND NO ONE'S GOING TO STOP ME!" This principle of trying something **passionately** can be applied to any activity, object, or concept.

My father, the greatest man I know, is **passionate** about being as productive as possible. He's **passionate** about providing a comfortable, safe, active life for his immediate and extended families. My father entered the navy at age 17 and served as an aviation electrician on the *Midway* and the *Kitty Hawk*, where he worked on F4 Phantom fighter jets. For him, it was a little boy's dream come true! He served his country with a zealous **passion**. The navy also taught him the work ethics needed to run a successful business. Everyone who knows my dad can say that he considers working playing. He's simply **passionate** about getting things done and done right. He gets to play with tools and build things and **passionately** enjoy his job while continuing to run a tight ship. It was while he was in the navy that he realized how much can be accomplished in one day. Realize that you have 24 hours a day and you can decide to use those 24 hours wisely. Start with a plan, make a list so that you can accomplish your undertakings—whether work or play—and do it all with vigorous **passion**.

My father's a rare breed. Since leaving the navy, he has built a highly successful electrical contracting corporation in California. He's performed countless jobs for TESLA, Intel, Google, DreamWorks, Kellogg's, and many other elites. His **passion** is doing the job and doing it well. "Make me fast and accurate" is his mantra. When he reached about 50 years old and his knees were completely wrecked from all the treacherous, endless play—I mean *work*—he had done, he realized that his **passion** lay elsewhere. Something was missing, so he sent my coworker and me down to Morro Bay, California, to search for a fishing boat he could purchase. We found the perfect one for him: a 1912 double-ender, single-screw Douglas fir fixer-upper. I saw it and said, "That's my dad's boat." Looking at it for the first time was similar to looking at Charlie Brown's Christmas tree; it needed not only a great deal of work but also a great deal of continuous maintenance. A playground on the water, in my dad's eyes. He conducted his research, as well as his networking. He customized his boat and fixed all the kinks. He planned and planned for his **passion**, his first trip out on the ocean. He lost sleep dreaming of being on the ocean—he lost sleep over something he didn't have to do but desperately wanted to. He opened a business. It's become not only his hobby but also his **passion**. He's a happier man because of it. He recently started playing the guitar too and is exceptional. He plays until his fingers bleed. He looks forward to playing his guitar. He's exceptional at electrical, fishing, and guitar for what reason, reader? He's **passionate** about them! In each instance, he started from scratch with an idea that he had searched for and discovered. He conducted the research, and new ideas arose with his discoveries, and he made his attempts enthusiastically and intelligently. He tried again and again, thus developing a good practice. He's now exceptional at all his **passions**.

*Give this some thought.*
*Write down one interest in your life that others*
*may consider work but you consider play.*

*This one interest (simple or grand) could be developed into a passion. It could even be developed into the path you take in life. Expand on what you have written down. Love it. Nurture it. Be passionate about it!*

My current **passion** is writing this guide. I have faith that it will lead me somewhere. I'm not looking for fame or fortune, although fortune would be nice; I'm looking for myself—**passionately** trying to see where I stand in this world. I'm writing what I know and **discovering** so much. I have faith that this will lead me somewhere. That "somewhere" is currently a mystery, but I've been **passionately** searching myself to see where I am and where I might go. As I started to search, I knew I would be discovering new and exciting things. What I didn't realize was that in writing this guide, I was being led to create a brand new me. The path to the new and ever-changing me was right in front of me. This path led me to the pages of this book. Practicing these 12 skills has changed my life, and I should continue changing for the better every day. I am mentally and physically striving to practice these skills with a vigorous, wild **passion**. I know that this is my current path, and it will ultimately lead me to my future path. It's almost magic, but it isn't. It's magic only in the sense that if you do what you like **passionately** and to its full extent, something good will come of it. It's not magic since it takes time and effort and a timeline. Life has no musical montages where you suddenly master a skill or task when you want to. It takes constant steps in the direction you want to go. Again, you're going to have to motivate yourself through tasks you don't necessarily want to fulfill to achieve your goal. I once asked my dad what the most difficult factor about owning a business is. He told me that it's "getting up every single day and doing it." He has no boss; he has only himself and the **loving** support of his wife, family, and friends. Treat yourself as your own boss when it comes to your **passion.** You should be counting down the seconds until you get to play again. Remember in elementary school when you stared at the clock, waiting for recess to begin? You used to be **passionate** about this. You used to be **passionate** about playing, imagining, **creating**, and having a good laugh. Where did this enthusiasm go? The pain of maturing probably occurred, but you don't have to stop playing. I'll tell you right now that hide-and-go-seek is a great game that can be played at any age.

My elementary school didn't have much grass, but it had paved asphalt. We called it the "blacktop." Because of the oils from the asphalt, I would come home covered head to toe in sweat, blood, snot, oil, and grease. Why? Because I played. I played **passionately**. I couldn't wait to get onto that blistering hot black asphalt and **passionately** try my best for the glory to be won playing with my friends. Somewhere down the line, some of us lose this **passion**, but I assure you that it can be found again. It takes escaping that deep pit of despair that only you can get yourself out of and trying the things that you used to like or trying the things that you have never tried until you find what you like, then **love**, and then are **passionate** about.

Each of the 12 skills in this handbook should be adopted **passionately** for them to have lasting, demonstrable effects.

As a final note on **passion**, follow your nose. Follow your gut. Follow your instincts. Follow your heart. Follow your **passion.** If you do all this, you will find something you never thought you would—true and lasting peace—and it is magical.

Thank you kindly, gentle reader. Now, go get 'em, champion.

# A Friendly Reminder

Living your **passion** is a combination of doing something you're good at and doing something you enjoy. Believe in yourself as you try all that you can—with maximal effort—and you may find that you have many **passions**. Your **passionate** efforts toward your goal should be enjoyable. If you do your best to develop your **passions**, then you will surely look forward to each day with a spirit of adventure. Follow your heart. It wants to lead you to someone special: the new, authentic, **passionate** you!

## Final Notes to the Gentle Reader

Read *The Four Agreements* by Don Miguel Ruiz.

It changed my life.

Use a computer or smartphone, and log on to MeetUp. It's an app that allows you to choose an activity that you're interested in, and it generates a list of upcoming events or gatherings based on that interest, such as arts and crafts, book clubs, cycling, philosophy, and volunteering, all of which you can join to meet others with similar interests.

## A Champion's Log

# Contact Me

## Email

abraatenselfhelp@gmail.com

**Facebook** https://www.facebook.com/
abraatenselfhelp

On Facebook, you can join a group discussion about this book as well!

Here is the list of different activities I find to be helpful for mental health.

Archery
 Badminton
 Baking
 Barbequing
 Basket-weaving
 Basketball
 Bathing
 Bird-watching
 Breathing
 Bug-hunting
 Bungee-jumping
 Calling a friend
 Camping
 Carving
 Cleaning up the roads
 Cleaning your house
 Cleaning your belongings
 Climbing
 Climbing a tree
 Complimenting yourself
 Cooking
 Counting to 100
 Crafting from scratch
 Crocheting
 Crosswords
 Darts
 Disc-golfing
 Doing a science experiment
 Donating your old items
 Drawing
 Drinking tea
 Driving
 Examining your hands
 Exploring nature

Expressing yourself
Finger-painting
Flying a kite
Forging
Geocaching
Getting a haircut
Getting a pet
Getting some food
Going outside
Going on a day trip
Going to a pay-to-pick
orchard
Going to a sauna
Golfing
Guitar-playing
Having a bonfire with friends
Having company over
Jacks
Jewelry-making
Jogging
Journaling
Juggling
Jumping rope
Knife-forging
Knitting
Lifting weights
Listening to music
Looking up jokes
Lovemaking
Making paper airplanes
Making some s'mores
Martial arts
Meditating
Origami
Painting
Painting rocks
Pampering yourself
Paying respect to the dead
Picnicking at the park

Ping-pong
Planting something
Playing a board game
Playing a card game
Playing catch
Playing piano
Playing with mud
Pool
Pottery
Pull-ups, push-ups, and
squats
Pulling weeds
Reading
Rearranging your closet
Reciting your mantras
Relaxing outdoors
Researching a subject
Restoring or repurposing
Riding a bike
Rock-hunting
Rock-tumbling
Rollerblading
Running
Sewing
Showering
Singing
Skateboarding
Skating
Skydiving
Stargazing
Sudoku
Surfing
Swimming
Taking a class
Taking pictures
Tending to your pets
Tennis
Thrift-shopping
Throwing a boomerang

Video-chatting with an old
friend
Video-gaming
Volunteering help to others
Walking
Walking barefoot
Watching "how to..."
videos
Watching something
wholesome or
informative
Water balloon fight
Whittling
Writing a short story
Yo-yo
Yodeling
Yoga

# Don't miss out!

Visit the website below and you can sign up to receive emails whenever Anthony Jacob Braaten publishes a new book. There's no charge and no obligation.

https://books2read.com/r/B-A-PDVK-HNUGB

**BOOKS 2 READ**

Connecting independent readers to independent writers.

## About the Author

As a patient to patient, human to human, Anthony Braaten despite his diagnosis of Bipolar I, ADHD, PTSD, an episode of psychosis, anxiety, depression, and a multitude of other mental illnesses has reached success. He adapted to his life only 12 skills he found if he practiced, would bring him lasting joy and peace. Join him taking you through these 12 skills and discover the authentic you that you want to be. Discover your passion and purpose in life. Discover yourself as you search deep within and rid yourself of all negativity. He wants to work with you and help you self-help yourself into being the person you always dreamed of.

www.ingramcontent.com/pod-product-compliance
Lightning Source LLC
Chambersburg PA
CBHW051212160726
47994CB00002B/577